Communication Research
and Broadcasting No. 7

Editor:
Internationales Zentralinstitut
für das Jugend- und Bildungsfernsehen (IZI)

Children and Families Watching Television

A Bibliography of Research on Viewing Processes

Compiled by
Werner Müller and Manfred Meyer

K·G·Saur
München · New York · London · Paris 1985

Editor of the series:
Internationales Zentralinstitut für das Jugend- und Bildungsfernsehen

Editor of this issue:
Manfred Meyer

Editorial assistant:
Rosemarie Hagemeister

Address of editor and editorial staff:
Internationales Zentralinstitut für das Jugend- und Bildungsfernsehen
Rundfunkplatz 1, D-8000 München 2
Telephone (089)5900-2140, Telex 52107-0 brm d

CIP-Kurztitelaufnahme der Deutschen Bibliothek

Müller, Werner:
Children and families watching television :
a bibliogr. of research on viewing processes
/ comp. by Werner Müller and Manfred Meyer. –
München ; New York ; London : Paris : Saur,
1985.
(Communication research and broadcasting ;
No. 7)
Dt. Ausg. u.d.T.: Müller, Werner: Kind und
Familie vor dem Bildschirm
ISBN 3-598-20206-7
NE: Meyer, Manfred:; HST; GT

© 1985 by K. G. Saur Verlag K. G., München
Phototypesetting by Fotosatz H. Buck, 8300 Kumhausen
Printed in the Federal Republic of Germany
by grafik + druck GmbH & Co., München
ISBN 3-598-20206-7

Contents

Preliminary remarks and notes for the user

On the subject of this bibliography

In this bibliography, we have compiled references to empirical research that seeks to clarify the nature of the television viewing process. This means we have particularly tried to trace all those studies that investigate the mental processes and interpersonal communications that occur when children − alone, with their siblings, peers, mothers, or within the family − turn their attention to the television screen.

Generally speaking, we have included research work that in our annotations and in some German literature is referred to as *reception research* ("Rezeptionsforschung"), a term which is here being increasingly applied to special areas of media consumption and which was originally used, for example, in connection with philological studies on literature reception (cf. *Charlton* and *Neumann, 1982;* entry No. 138 of this volume).

The common denominators, as it were, of this type of research are at least twofold: it is primarily recipient-orientated (as opposed to content- or effect-orientated) and it emphasizes the predominantly active role the recipient plays in whatever form of interaction with the media.

In accordance with our objectives as an information and documentation centre attached to a broadcasting house, our particular interest in this research area − apart from its being a relatively new and complex approach which in itself is worth being followed up and documented − results from the fact that the principal research questions are similar to the questions asked by the producers and editors of television programmes. They are obviously more and more interested in whether their products are being paid attention to − for example, in competition with the programme output of competing channels −, whether they are comprehended with regard to both contents and media language, whether the characters or actions portrayed are perceived as what they are meant to be, in short, whether the programmes are properly 'received', particularly by the child audience. On the other hand, the awareness of traditional approaches and findings of effects research is often felt to belong to a different level of responsibility, e.g. that of programme planning and programme policy.

In fact, the literature compiled here is to a large extent the outcome of a development which can be described as a shift of emphasis away from the traditional research into media effects to what is called here reception research. The 'classical' effects research worked out a large number of con-

6

nections between the programme contents and their medium- or long-term effects on the viewer. In so doing, certain mental processes that occur during the reception of television programmes were neglected to a certain extent, or it was implied that this reception process was relatively stable and invariable. This approach came up against some limits especially with regard to the accuracy and the predictive validity of the findings about the effects of television on children.

The basic idea behind the approach of effects research is plausible: the central issue is whether a particular programme content, a programme type, a presentational form or a single formal feature have obvious and predictable effects on the recipient. It is easy to comprehend the interest which gave rise to such a question, at least on the part of any producer of televised messages with persuasive intent: effects which are as clear as possible on the largest possible number of viewers are expected, otherwise there is no point in using and paying for the mass medium television. On the other side, there is the concern of the public, or rather of a certain type of its opinion leaders who are indefatigable in warning against the harmful and detrimental effects of television – as has been the case with every new technical invention, one might add.

With regard to research into the influence ascribed to television, especially in the case of children, it was and still is in many studies chiefly a matter of the medium- and long-term effects of the commercials, the effect of violence on the screen, especially in the entertainment programmes for adults so popular with children, and also of the intended long-term effects of certain children's series with prosocial contents or educational objectives.

The findings are heterogeneous, in some cases even contradictory. All attempts to establish clear causal relationships or even to predict long-term effects give rise to difficulties. Efforts to achieve scientific exactness, for example by considering the demands of representativeness and replicability, did not solve the problem, but made it more difficult to develop meaningful models and to transfer the findings into the area of application.

The principal features of reception research

Examination of the reception processes, which is the central theme of this bibliography, brings certain phenomena into the limelight which have been neglected by research into television effects. The research interest is focused, on the one hand, on the active involvement (or lack of it) which the viewer brings to the communication process. The child watching television is recognized more and more as an active participant, whose behaviour towards the medium is determined by seeking, selecting or even rejecting the information or messages presented, and whose activity can give rise to effects quite different from the negative ones expected or the positive ones hoped for.

On the other hand, the significance of factors had been recognized which could also provide explanations for different effects by one and the same programme. Researchers became more and more interested in the intervening variables in the communication process, which form, as it were, the constituent elements of the reception process and which were identified while considering the conditions of the viewing situation, the cognitive and emotional predispositions of the recipient, his personal way of processing the information he is confronted with, and the interaction with his social environment.

This social environment, which comprises, above all, other members of the family, friends, peers, siblings and adults also watching the programme and commenting on it, is now known to have a crucial influence on the reception process and has became another focus of research interest.

The differentiation of the problems goes hand in hand with a refinement and diversification of research models:
- Participatory observation, natural setting and field research are gaining acceptance.
- Smaller design units are being chosen. More information is being obtained from a smaller number of subjects.
- The statements are generalized with regard to smaller, narrowly defined target groups.
- Formative research makes possible a close connection between researchers and producers.
- The findings are often subjected to an evaluation, e.g. to a systematic secondary analysis of the data or to a reconsideration on the basis of methodological criticism.

Subdivisions and chapters

To help the user to obtain an overall picture and to find his way through the bibliographical material it has been arranged along pragmatic lines. The division into 13 chapters, which in their turn constitute the four parts, is to be understood as a facet-like arrangement which resulted from the sifting and ordering of the references. It can be assumed, however, that this division reflects the main points of emphasis and fields of research interest.

Part I contains basic bibliographical material for study and more extensive literature searches (Chapter 1) as well as introductions, literature reviews, general papers, and publications with textbook or reader character of a more recent date which lead up to the individual problems of the research areas in question (Chapter 2).

The literature collated in Part II deals with individual aspects of the reception process. This includes all the mental processes which a child uses to transform reality as presented on television into his own ideas: excitement, emotional reactions, processes of attention, comprehension and cognition, discrimination between fiction and reality, social perception and media literacy.

Part III deals with the social aspects of reception, i.e. all the behaviour patterns and the social interactions of viewers which can be observed during viewing: the viewing behaviour of the child, what happens between parents and children, and the influence of parents or other coviewing adults and peers on the reception process.

Part IV (Chapter 13) includes the studies and material on aspects of application of the research dealt with so far. Media education refers to any attempts to enable children to handle the medium of television and its messages in an appropriate way.

The following annotations to the individual chapters are by no means to be understood as definitions of the various research fields. We only intend to explain the rationale underlying the structure of this compilation.

Attention (Chapter 3):
The child actively pays a frequently changing degree of attention to his environment and thus to television. Which media contents reach the child and how these are assimilated by him or her in each particular case, depends on the degree and type of attention. The attention is directed partly by the formal features of the programme and partly by environmental stimuli or by interests. The studies listed here report on processes of observable and latent attention, frequently with regard to processes of understanding and short-term memory.

Comprehension (Chapter 4):
Comprehension, as distinct from the cognitive processes dealt with in the next chapter, involves the question of how children assimilate the different formats and formal features of television presentations, and how at the same time they grasp the sense of the individual contents and messages.

Arousal and Emotions (Chapter 5):
The reception process is influenced by the emotional state the child is in while he or she is viewing. This state is frequently, but not always, determined by the programme contents. A large number of emotional states and feelings are involved, e.g. anxiety, fear, pleasure, humour, tension, relaxation.

Cognition (Chapter 6):
Here the research literature is to be found on all the processes of perception, of cognition and of recognition, if these have not been assigned to one of the three chapters that follow. Some of the phenomena considered here are: information acquisition, information processing, perceptional schemata, perceptional style, spatial perception, time perception, velocity perception, etc.

Fantasy and Reality (Chapter 7):
The literature collated in this chapter deals with the child's ability to assess the relation of the media contents to reality, in other words to discriminate between fictitious presentations and the presentation of reality. Here the following cognitive processes with regard to the child are significant: discrimination, imagination, reality perception.

Social Perception (Chapter 8):
This chapter contains the literature on the question of how children perceive the social interactions presented on television. This includes person perception, perception of stereotypes, role perception, attribution, social competence, identification, etc.

Media Literacy (Chapter 9):
Turning attention to the cognitive processes has given rise to the question of whether media-specific abilities or skills are necessary for viewing television which, as they develop, will make a more competent use of the media possible. In this chapter the research literature has been compiled on a topic which is dealt with in English-speaking countries under the headings of 'viewership skills', 'media literacy', 'literate viewing' and 'critical viewing skills', 'receivership skills', etc. Here some of the theoretical fundamentals of media education are also to be found (cf. Chapter 13).

Viewing Behaviour (Chapter 10):
In this chapter the research into the child's visible, observable behaviour while viewing is collated (e.g. eye movements, gestures, facial expressions, speaking the text, singing the songs, parasocial interactions with the programme contents), inasfar as these references have not been assigned to other chapters, in particular Chapters 5 ("Arousal and Emotions"), 3 ("Attention"), 11 ("Parental Influence and the Family") or 12 ("Peers").

Parental Influence and the Family (Chapter 11):
This chapter covers all the events in the family during viewing: interpersonal communication between the child and one or both parents; familial interaction and communication; the influence of family members on attention, comprehension, information processing and viewing behaviour.

Peers (Chapter 12):
This chapter treats the research into the interactions of peers and siblings during viewing. (Unless our search for material has been inadequate, the small quantity of literature collated in this chapter indicates that this is a neglected area of research.)

Media Education (Chapter 13):
Here a very wide range of approaches for influencing children's reception processes are collected. The idea that children can 'learn to view television' forms, as it were, the common denominator. The aim throughout is to increase the child's competence, and to strengthen desirable and to prevent undesirable media effects. Not only evalutive studies of media education projects were included in this chapter, but also descriptions of practice-related projects from school, home, pre-school and kindergarten.

Selection criteria; notes for the user

In accordance with what has been said above, this bibliography contains mainly references to empirical studies covering children aged from about 2 to 12 years, their behaviour as recipients of television programmes and the personal and familial interactions while viewing, as well as literature reviews, research reviews or comprehensive summaries of the research areas in question.

We have therefore not taken into consideration:
— studies on correlations between social or individual characteristics and viewing habits of children, their media usage or their attitudes towards television;
— studies of the events which occurred *before* the television was switched on and which influence programme preference or programme selection outside of the family context;
— studies which, without considering the viewing process itself, analyse effects which took place *after* the television was switched off, e.g. studies on retention, recall, or short-term learning, on long-term effects of the media related to academic achievements, motivation, social behaviour, personality development, etc.;
— theoretical and methodological treatises, content analyses, critical and polemical considerations as well as general, popularizing works in which research evidence is occasionally referred to without being adequately substantiated.

Furthermore, the selection was restricted to research work published in the period of 1975 to about September 1985. Publications which appeared before

1975 can be found in other bibliographies cited below (Chapter 1), especially in the comprehensive, annotated research bibliography by *Comstock* and his associates (1975; see entries 3 to 5 in this volume).

Our bibliography contains only references to publications in English, French and German. For more extensive research the Institute would be pleased to provide information on other bibliographical sources, especially in European countries.

Another criterion for selection was the availability or accessibility of pertinent literature. As a rule, the compilers had the original documents at their disposal. In general, we excluded references to almost inaccessible literature, i.e. unpublished manuscripts and dissertations, conference papers, working papers and the like, if they are not obtainable through the ERIC Reproduction Service. Whenever possible, we mentioned the accession number of ERIC documents included here (Arlington, Va.: ERIC ED...). They can be ordered in the form of either hard copies or (very much cheaper) microfiches from: ERIC Documents Reproduction Service, P.O. Box 190, Arlington, Virginia 22210, U.S.A.

There are, however, numerous institutions in all parts of the world that store ERIC material and offer reproduction services. They are listed in the 'Directory of ERIC Microfiche Collections', published by the National Institute of Education, Washington, D.C. It is available from: ERIC Processing and Reference Facility, 4833 Rugby Avenue, Suite 303, Bethesda, Maryland 20814, U.S.A.

This bibliography is the English version of the German-language publication entitled "Kind und Familie vor dem Bildschirm. Eine Bibliographie ausgewählter Forschungsergebnisse zur Fernsehrezeption", which has just appeared in our series *Bibliographischer Dienst* (vol. 5; München: Saur 1985, 149 p., ISBN 3-598-20685-2). This explains the somewhat unusual format of the individual entries.

As far as this format is concerned, we have followed the rules for machine-readable description of bibliographical references established by a working group of German documentation centres (Dokumentationsring Pädagogik – DOPAED), of which we are a member. According to these rules journal articles are cited with the title of the journal, volume number/year/issue number, pages (for example: *Journal of Communication*, 25/1975/3, S. 114 – 126). If available, the ISBN No. has been given in the line following the place, printer or publisher, and date of publication. The German abbreviations in the last line refer to addenda to a document such as notes ('Anm.'), bibliographical references ('Bibl.'), tables ('Tab.') etc. They are listed and translated on page 13.

Documents with a cooperative authorship of more than three writers are listed under the subject title, followed by the authors who are referred to as "Mitarb.", i.e. collaborators. Cooperative editors such as research institutes, organizations, governmental bodies etc. also follow the subject titles. Within the individual chapters all citations have then been arranged in alphabetical order according to the name of the author mentioned first, or according to the subject title in cases mentioned above.

The descriptors used in this bibliography are translations of the keywords currently in use in the documentation department of our Institute. Wherever possible, we have used the equivalents to our descriptors in either the *Thesaurus of ERIC Descriptors* (10th Edition, 1984) or the *Thesaurus of Psychological Index Terms* (4th Edition, 1985).

Special acknowledgements are due to our collaborators in the Institute, especially to *Helga Weise-Richter* for effectively retrieving the documents, to *Gisela Duvigneau* for her troublesome labour with the entry formats, and to *Rosemarie Hagemeister* for editorial assistance, elaboration of the indexes and the finalization of the manuscript for print.

Manfred Meyer
Werner Müller

Munich, December 1985

German abbreviations in the entries:

Abb.	– illustrations	o.J.	– no date
Anh.	– appendix	o.O.	– no place
Aus	– from	o. Verl.	– no printer or publisher
Anm.	– notes	pres.	– presented
deutsch	– German	Red.	– editor, editing dept.
Bibl.	– bibliography, references	Reg.	– index
engl.	– English	Res.	– abstract
franz.	– French	S.	– page(s)
Gph.	– graphs	span.	– Spanish
Hrsg.	– editor	Tab.	– tables
Kt.	– map	u.a.	– et al.
Mitarb.	– collaborator	Vorr.	– author of editorial

Part I: Bibliographies, Introductory Literature

Chapter 1: Bibliographies

1
Children and advertising. An annotated bibliography.
Meringoff, Laurene (Hrsg.)
Council of Better Business Bureaus (Hrsg.)
New York, N.Y.: Children's Advertising Review Unit 1980. 96 S.
(Arlington, Va.: ERIC ED 196 019.)
Bibl.: Reg.

Advertising; Bibliography; Children; Effects Research; Media Policy;
Television

2
Children and television. An abstract bibliography.
ERIC Clearinghouse on Early Childhood Education, Urbana, Ill. (Hrsg.)
Urbana, Ill.: Publications Office, IREC, College of Education, Univ. of
Illinois 1975. 54 S.
Bibl.

Bibliography; Children; Television; United States

3
Comstock, George; Fisher, Marilyn
Television and human behavior. A guide to the pertinent scientific
literature.
Rand Corporation, Santa Monica, Calif. (Hrsg.)
Santa Monica, Calif.: Rand 1975. IX, 344 S.
Bibl.; Reg.; Tab.

Adolescents; Bibliography; Children; Communicator Research;
Media Research; Minority; Recipient Research; Television; United States

4
Comstock, George
Television and human behavior. The key studies.
Christen, F.G. (Mitarb.); Fisher, M.L. (Mitarb.); Quarles, R.C. (Mitarb.)
u.a.
Rand Corporation, Santa Monica, Calif. (Hrsg.)
Santa Monica, Calif.: Rand 1975. IX, 251 S.
Bibl.; Reg.

Bibliography; Media Research; Research Methodology; Television;
United States

5
Comstock, George; Lindsey, Georg
Television and human behavior. The research horizon, future and present.
Rand Corporation, Santa Monica, Calif. (Hrsg.)
Santa Monica, Calif.: Rand 1975. IX, 120 S.
Bibl.; Tab.

Bibliography; Literature Reviews; Media Research; Research Methodology;
Socialization; Television; United States

6
CTW research bibliography. Research papers relating to the Children's
Television Workshop and its experimental educational series: 'Sesame
Street' and 'The Electric Company' 1968 – 76.
Children's Television Workshop, New York, N.Y. (Hrsg.)
New York, N.Y.: CTW, Research Division o.J. (ca. 1977). 20 S.

Bibliography; Children's Television; Reading; "Sesame Street";
United States

7
Dumrauf, Klaus
Vorschulfernsehen und Kleinkinder. Eine kommentierte Bibliographie.
Berlin: Spiess 1979. 400 S.
(Hochschul-Skripten: Medien. 10)

Bibliography; Children's Television; Compilations; Literature Reviews;
Preschool Children; Television

8
Fairman, Edith M.
Television violence and its effects on children. A selected annotated
bibliography.
Library of Congress, Washington, D.C. (Hrsg.)
Washington, D.C.: Library of Congress 1976. 24 S.
(Congressional research service.)
Bibl.

Bibliography; Children; Television; United States; Violent Content

9
Gordon, Thomas F.; Verna, Mary Ellen
Mass communication effects and processes. A comprehensive bibliography,
1950 – 1975.
Beverly Hills, Calif. u.a.: Sage 1978. 229 S.
ISBN 0-8039-0903-9
Bibl.; Reg.

Bibliography; Mass Communication; Mass Media Effects; Media Uses

10
Gordon, Thomas F.; Verna, Mary Ellen
Mass media and socialization. A selected bibliography.
School of Communications and Theater, Philadelphia (Hrsg.); Temple
University, Philadelphia (Hrsg.)
Philadelphia, Pa.: Temple University, Radio – Television – Film
Department 1973. 47 S.
(Communications research reports.)
Bibl.

*Bibliography; Communication Research; Mass Media; Mass Media
Effects; Media Uses; Social Norm; Social Role; Socialization; Values*

11
Lake, Sara
Television's impact on children and adolescents. A special interest resource
guide in education.
Phoenix, Ariz.: Oryx Press 1981. VIII, 102 S.
ISBN 0-912700-87-4
Bibl.; Reg.

*Adolescents; Bibliography; Children; Education; Effects Research;
Recipient Behavior; Television; Viewing Situation*

12

Mass media and socialization. International bibliography and different perspectives.
Halloran, James D. (Hrsg.)
International Association for Mass Communication Research (Hrsg.)
Leicester: International Association for Mass Communication Research
1976. 130 S.
Bibl.

Bibliography; Documentation; Mass Media; Socialization; Theoretical Criticism

13

Meyer, Manfred; Nissen, Ursula
Bibliographie zu Sesame Street.
In: Fernsehen und Bildung, 10/1976/1 – 2, S. 134 – 146.

Bibliography; Children's Television; "Sesame Street"; Television; United States

14

Meyer, Manfred; Nissen, Ursula
Effects and functions of television: children and adolescents. A bibliography of selected research literature 1970 – 1978.
Internationales Zentralinstitut für das Jugend- und Bildungsfernsehen, München (Hrsg.)
München u.a.: Saur 1979. 172 S.
(Communication research and broadcasting. 2)
Bibl.

Adolescents; Bibliography; Children; Effects Research; Media Uses

15

Meyer, Manfred; Nissen, Ursula
Wirkungen und Funktionen des Fernsehens: Kinder und Jugendliche. Eine Bibliographie ausgewählter Forschungsliteratur der Jahre 1970 – 1976.
Internationales Zentralinstitut für das Jugend- und Bildungsfernsehen, München (Hrsg.)
München: IZI 1977. 147 S.
(Bibliographischer Dienst.1)
Bibl.

Adolescents; Bibliography; Children; Effects Research; Media Uses

16
Murray, John P.; Nayman, Oguz B.; Atkin, Charles K.
Television and the child. A comprehensive research bibliography.
In: Journal of Broadcasting, 16/1971 – 72/1, S. 3 – 20.
Bibl.; Anm.

Bibliography; Children; Effects Research; Program Contents; Television;
Viewing Behavior; Violent Content

17
Murray, John P.
Television and youth. 25 years of research and controversy.
Siegel, Alberta E. (Vorr.)
Boys Town, Neb. u.a.: The Boys Town Center for the Study of Youth
Development 1980. 278 S.
ISBN 0-938510-00-2
Bibl.

Bibliography; Children; Educational Television; Effects Research;
Literature Reviews; Political Socialization; Prosocial Content; Reception
Processes; Recipient Behavior; Television; Television Advertising; Violent
Content; Youth

18
Weber, David M.
The effects of critical television viewing in educating primary students. An
annotated bibliography.
South Bend, Ind.: Indiana Univ. 1982. 38 S.
(Arlington, Va.: ERIC ED 218 011.)
Bibl.

Bibliography; Children; Media Education; Media Literacy; Television

Chapter 2: Literature Reviews, Compilations, Readers

19
Anderson, Daniel R.; Bryant, Jennings
Research on children's television viewing. The state of the art.
In: Children's understanding of television.
Bryant, Jennings (Hrsg.) u.a.
New York, N.Y. u.a.: Academic Press 1983, S. 331 – 353.
Bibl.; Gph.

Attention; Children; Literature Reviews; Program Output; Program Preferences; Recipient Behavior; Recipient Research; Television; Viewing Behavior; Viewing Situation

20
Bergler, Reinhold; Six, Ulrike
Psychologie des Fernsehens. Wirkungsmodelle und Wirkungseffekte unter besonderer Berücksichtigung der Wirkung auf Kinder und Jugendliche.
Bern u.a.: Huber 1979. 302 S.
(Beiträge zur empirischen Sozialforschung.)
Bibl.

Adolescents; Children; Communication Research; Effects Research; Literature Reviews; Television

21
Bonfadelli, Heinz
Die Sozialisationsperspektive in der Massenkommunikationsforschung.
Neue Ansätze, Methoden und Resultate zur Stellung der Massenmedien im Leben der Kinder und Jugendlichen.
Berlin: Spiess 1981. 427 S.
(Beiträge zur Medientheorie und Kommunikationsforschung. 20)
ISBN 3-88435-035-8
Bibl.; Anm.; Abb.; Tab.; Gph.

Adolescents; Children; Communications; Economy; Family; Mass Communication; Media Research; Political Socialization; School; Socialization Research; Society; Theoretical Criticism

22
Cantor, Joanne R.
Research on television's effects on children.
In: Phaedrus, 5/1978/1, S. 9–13.
Bibl.; Abb.

*Children; Distraction; Effects Research; Imitation; Introductory
Literature; Television; Violent Content*

23
Chalvon, Mireille; Corset, Pierre; Souchon, Michel
L'enfant devant la télévision.
Tournai: Casterman 1979. 184 S.
(Collection "E3".)
ISBN 2-203-20252-1
Bibl.

Children; France; Mass Media Effects; Media Pedagogics; Television

24
Children and television.
Brown, Ray (Hrsg.)
London: Collier Macmillan 1976. 368 S.
Bibl.

*Audiences; Children; Children's Television; Effects Research; Family;
Social Learning; Television; Television Commercials; Viewing Behavior;
Violent Content*

25
Children and the faces of television. Teaching, violence, selling.
Palmer, Edward L. (Hrsg.); Dorr, Aimée (Hrsg.)
New York, N.Y. u.a.: Academic Press 1980. XI, 360 S.
ISBN 0-12-544480-X
Bibl.; Reg.; Tab.; Gph.

*Children; Children's Television; Communication Research; Compilations;
Educational Television; Mass Media Effects; Program Contents; Television
Advertising; Violent Content*

26
Children and the formal features of television. Approaches and findings
of experimental and formative research.
Meyer, Manfred (Hrsg.)
Internationales Zentralinstitut für das Jugend- und Bildungsfernsehen,
München (Hrsg.)
München u.a.: Saur 1983. 333 S.
(Communication research and broadcasting. 6)
ISBN 3-598-20205-9
Bibl.; Anm.; Abb.; Tab.; Gph.

*Children; Compilations; Effects Research; Formal Features; Formative
Education; Media Literacy; Recipient Research; Television*

27
Children communicating. Media and development of thought, speech and
understanding.
Wartella, Ellen (Hrsg.)
Beverly Hills, Calif. u.a.: Sage 1979. 286 S.
(Sage annual reviews of communication research. 7)
ISBN 0-8039-1171-8
Bibl.; Tab.; Gph.

*Children; Cognitive Development; Communication Research;
Compilations; Mass Media Effects; Perceptual Development; Speech
Development*

28
Children's understanding of television. Research on attention and
comprehension.
Bryant, Jennings (Hrsg.); Anderson, Daniel R. (Hrsg.)
New York, N.Y.: Academic Press 1983. XIV, 370 S.
ISBN 0-12-138160-9
Bibl.; Reg.; Tab.; Gph.

*Attention; Children; Compilations; Comprehension; Information
Processing; Media Literacy; Reception Processes; Recipient Research;
Television; Viewing Behavior*

29
Collins, W. Andrew; Korać, N.
Recent progress in the study of the effects of television viewing on social
development.

In: International Journal of Behavioral Development, 5/1982/ – ,
S. 171 – 193.
Bibl.

*Children; Comprehension; Effects Research; Literature Reviews; Media
Functions; Social Behavior; Television*

30
Comstock, George
Television and human behavior. The key studies.
Christen, F.G. (Mitarb.); Fisher, M.L. (Mitarb.); Quarles, R.C. (Mitarb.)
u.a.
Rand Corporation, Santa Monica, Calif. (Hrsg.)
Santa Monica, Calif.: Rand 1975. IX, 251 S.
Bibl.; Reg.

*Bibliography; Media Research; Research Methodology; Television; United
States*

31
Comstock, George; Lindsey, Georg
Television and human behavior. The research horizon, future and present.
Rand Corporation, Santa Monica, Calif. (Hrsg.)
Santa Monica, Calif.: Rand 1975. IX, 120 S.
Bibl.; Tab.

*Bibliography; Literature Reviews; Media Research; Research Methodology;
Socialization; Television; United States*

32
Corset, Pierre
Fernsehen im Leben französischer Kinder. Ein Überblick über neue
Forschungsansätze.
In: Wie verstehen Kinder Fernsehprogramme?
Meyer, Manfred (Hrsg.)
München u.a.: Saur 1984, S. 178 – 198.
Bibl.

*Attitude Formation; Children; France; Literature Reviews; Media Literacy;
Reality Perception; Recall; Reception Processes; Television; Viewing
Situation*

33
Corset, Pierre
Television in the lives of French children. A review of recent research.
In: Children and the formal features of television.
Meyer, Manfred (Hrsg.)
München u.a.: Saur 1983, S. 188–208.
Bibl.

Attitude Formation; Children; France; Literature Reviews; Media Literacy;
Reality Perception; Recall; Reception Processes; Television; Viewing
Situation

34
Cullingford, Cedric
Children and television.
Hampshire: Gower 1984. X, 239 S.
ISBN 0-566-00655-3
Bibl.; Reg.

Children; Expectation; Interviews; Learning; Mass Media Effects;
Program Preferences; Recipient Behavior; Recipient Research; Television;
United Kingdom; United States

35
Dorr, Aimée
When I was a child I thought as a child.
In: Television and social behavior.
Withey, Stephan B. (Hrsg.) u.a.
Hillsdale, N.J.: Erlbaum 1980, S. 191–230.
Bibl.; Anm.; Tab.

Attribution; Children; Cognitive Processes; Media Psychology; Person
Perception; Reality Perception; Reception Processes; Role Perception;
Social Perception; Television; Theory Formulation

36
The effects of television advertising on children. Review and
recommendations.
Adler, Richard P. (Mitarb.); Lesser, Gerald S. (Mitarb.); Meringoff,
Laurene Krasny (Mitarb.) u.a.

Lexington, Mass u.a.: Lexington Books 1981. XI, 367 S.
ISBN 0-669-02814-2
Bibl.; Anm.; Tab.; Gph.

Children; Compilations; Effects Research; Television; Television Commercials; United States

37
Les enfants et la télévision.
Hubert, Pauline (Mitarb.); Smets, Joël (Mitarb.); Malrain, Eric (Mitarb.) u.a.
Radio – Télévision Belge de la Communauté Française, Bruxelles (Hrsg.)
Bruxelles: RTBF 1985. XXII, 177 S.
Bibl.; Tab.; Gph.

Adolescents; Belgium; Children; Children's Television; Compilations; Europe; Family; Television

38
Familie und Fernsehen. Neueste Ergebnisse der Fernsehforschung und deren Konsequenzen für die Programmarbeit.
Frank, Bernward (Mitarb.); Kellner, Hella (Mitarb.); Horn, Imme (Mitarb.) u.a.
Zweites Deutsches Fernsehen, Mainz (Hrsg.)
Mainz: ZDF 1978, 55 S.
(ZDF-Schriftenreihe. 21)
Bibl.; Anm.

Attitudes; Family; Parents; Ratings; Socialization; Television

39
Feilitzen, Cecilia von; Filipson, Leni; Schyller, Ingela
Open your eyes to children's viewing. On children, television and radio now and in the future.
Swedish Broadcasting Corporation, Stockholm, Audience and Programme Research Department (Hrsg.)
Stockholm: Swedish Broadcasting Corporation, Audience and Programme Research Department 1979. 134 S.
Bibl., Anm.

Broadcast Media; Children's Television; Mass Media Effects; Recipient Research; Sweden; Television

40
Fosarelli, Patricia D.
Television and children. A review.
In: Developmental and Behavioral Pediatrics, 5/1984/1, S. 30–37.
Bibl.

Children; Comprehension; Effects Research; Literature Reviews; Parent Influence; Program Contents; Television; Televiewing Frequency

41
Fowles, Barbara R.
A child and his television set. What is the nature of the relationship?
In: Education and Urban Society, 10/1977/1, S. 89–103.
Bibl.

Children; Effects Research; Introductory Literature; Reception Processes; "Sesame Street"; Television

42
Fritz, Angela
Die Familie in der Rezeptionssituation. Grundlage zu einem Situationskonzept für die Fernseh- und Familienforschung.
Zugl.: München, Univ., Diss., 1983.
München: Minerva-Publikation 1984. 276 S.
(Minerva-Fachserie Wirtschafts- und Sozialwissenschaften)
ISBN 3-597-10514-9
Bibl.; Anm.; Tab.; Gph.

Communication Theory; Family Relations; Literature Reviews; Research Design; Television; Viewing Situation

43
The future of children's television. Results of the Markle Foundation – Boys Town Conference.
Murray, John P. (Hrsg.); Salomon, Gavriel (Mitarb.); Morrisett, Lloyd N. (Vorr.) u.a.
Boys Town Center (Hrsg.); John and Mary R. Markle Foundation (Hrsg.)
Boys Town, Neb.: Father Flanagan's Boys' Home 1984. 174 S.
ISBN 0-9358510-05-3
Bibl.; Tab.; Gph.

Children; Communication Technology; Compilations; Conference Proceedings; Education; Introductory Literature; Prognosis; Television; United States

44
Haase, Henning
Kinder und Medien. Eine Literaturübersicht zur Wirkungsforschung 1975
bis 1979.
In: Media Perspektiven, − /1979/12, S. 797−810, 843−844.
Bibl.

Children; Cognition; Effects Research; Emotions; Literature Reviews;
Research Needs; Television; Television Advertising

45
Honig, Alice Sterling
Research in review. Television and young children.
In: Young Children, 38/1983/4, S. 63−76.
Bibl.

Aggressive Behavior; Effects Research; Infants; Learning Processes;
Literature Reviews; Preschool Children; Socialization; Television

46
Howe, Michael J.A.
Television and children.
London: New University Education 1977. 157 S.
Bibl.

Children; Effects Research; Instructional Television; Television; Viewing
Behavior; Violent Content

47
Hubert, Pauline
La télévision pour enfants.
Bruxelles: De Boeck 1981. 92 S.
(Univers des Sciences Humaines. 17)
Reg.; Gph.

Belgium; Children; Children's Television; Effects Research; Television;
Viewing Behavior

48
Huston-Stein, Aletha
Television and growing up. The medium gets equal time.
Paper presented at the Annual Meeting of the American Psychological
Association, 85th, San Francisco, Calif., August 26−30, 1977.
American Psychological Association (Hrsg.)

Lawrence, Kan.: Univ. of Kansas 1977. 28 S. (Arlington, Va.: ERIC ED 148 462.)
Bibl.

Attention; Children; Effects Research; Formal Features; Introductory Literature; Television; Violent Content

49
Jensen Klaus
Der kindliche Umgang mit Massenmedien. Handlungstheoretische und empirische Aspekte psychologischer Analysen.
In: Zeitschrift für Pädagogik, 26/1980/3, S. 383 – 399.
Bibl.; Anm.; Gph.

Action Approach; Children; Federal Republic of Germany; Introductory Literature; Mass Media; Media Uses; Reception Processes

50
Kinder vor dem Bildschirm.
Heygster, Anna-Luise (Hrsg.); Stolte, Dieter (Hrsg.)
Mainz: v. Hase und Köhler 1974. 240 S.
(Mainzer Tage der Fernsehkritik. 6)
ISBN 3-7758-0867-1
Bibl.; Tab.

Children's Television; Conference Proceedings; Federal Republic of Germany; Program Output; Television; Television Criticism

51
Kübler, Hans-Dieter
Kinder und Fernsehen. Ein Literaturbericht.
In: Fernsehforschung – Fernsehkritik.
Kreuzer, Helmut (Hrsg.)
Göttingen: Vandenhoeck und Ruprecht 1980, S. 136 – 204.
Bibl.

Children; Coverage; Family; Federal Republic of Germany; Literature Reviews; Mass Media Effects; Media Contents; Media Uses; Society; Television

52
Learning from television. Psychological and educational research.
Howe, Michael J.A. (Hrsg.); Bryant, Jennings (Mitarb.); Alexander, Alison F. (Mitarb.) u.a.

London u.a.: Academic Press 1983. XVI, 226 S.
ISBN 0-12-357160-X
Bibl.; Reg.; Tab.; Gph.

Children; Children's Advertising; Children's Television; Compilations; Educational Television; Learning; Media Education; Socialization; Television; Violent Content

53
Lesser, Gerald S.
Children and television. Lessons from Sesame Street.
Cooney, Joan Ganz (Vorr.); Morrisett, Lloyd (Vorr.)
New York, N.Y.: Random House 1974. XXVIII, 290 S.
ISBN 0-394-48100-3
Bibl.

Children's Television; Preschool Children; "Sesame Street"; Television

54
Lesser, Harvey
Television and the preschool child. A psychological theory of instruction and curriculum development.
New York, N.Y. u.a.: Academic Press 1977. X, 261 S.
(Educational psychology.)
Bibl.

Cognitive Development; Curriculum Development; Educational Psychology; Instructional Television; Literature Reviews; Preschool Children; "Sesame Street"; Speech Development; United States; Visual Perception

55
Maletzke, Gerhard
Kinder und Fernsehen.
In: Wie Kinder mit dem Fernsehen umgehen.
Sturm, Hertha (Hrsg.) u.a.
Stuttgart 1979, S. 21 – 83.
ISBN 3-12-930610-2
Bibl.; Anm.; Tab.

Children; Effects Research; Federal Republic of Germany; Literature Reviews; Recipient Research; Television

56
Moody, Kate
Growing up on television. A report to parents.
New York, N.Y. u.a.: McGraw-Hill 1984. 238 S.
ISBN 0-07-042871-9
Abb.; Bibl.; Reg.

Children; Effects Research; Introductory Literature; Television

57
Murray, John P.; Kippax, Susan
From the early window to the late night show.
International trends in the study of television's impact on children and
adults.
School of Behavioural Sciences, Sydney (Hrsg.); Australian Research
Grants Committee; Macquarie University Research Fund
Sydney: Macquarie Univ., School of Behavioural Sciences o.J. (1978 oder
1979). 74 S., 31 S. Anh.
(Television and socialization.)
Bibl.

Children; Effects Research; Everyday Life; Reality; Television

58
Murray, John P.
Television and youth. 25 years of research and controversy.
Siegel Alberta E. (Vorr.)
Boys Town, Neb. u.a.: The Boys Town Center for the Study of Youth
Development 1980. 278 S.
ISBN 0-938510-00-2
Bibl.

*Adolescents; Bibliography; Children; Educational Television; Effects
Research; Literature Reviews; Political Socialization; Prosocial Content;
Reception Processes; Recipient Behavior; Television Advertising; Violent
Content*

59
Murray, John P.: Kippax, Susan
Television's impact on children and adults. Interpersonal perspectives on
theory and research.
In: Mass communication review yearbook. 2.
Wilhoit, G. Cleveland (Hrsg.) u.a.

Beverly Hills, Calif.: Sage 1981, S. 582–638.
Bibl.; Tab.; Gph.

Adults; Children; Cross Cultural Studies; Effects Research; Everyday Life; Literature Reviews; Recipient Research; Television; Violent Content

60
Noble, Grant
Children in front of the small screen.
London: Constable; Beverly Hills, Calif. u.a.: Sage 1975, 256 S.
(Communication and society.)
ISBN 0-8039-0566-1
Bibl.; Reg.

Children; Deviations; Escapism; Identification; Mass Media Effects; Media Research; Person Perception; Research Methodology; Socialization; Television; Violent Content

61
Pearl, David
Violence and aggression.
In: Society, 21/1984/6, S. 17–22.

Attitude Change; Children; Mass Media Effects; Observational Learning; Television; Theory Comparison; Violent Content

62
Research on the effects of television advertising on children. A review of the literature and recommendations for future research.
Adler, Richard P. (Mitarb.); Friedlander, Bernard Z. (Mitarb.); Lesser, Gerald S. (Mitarb.) u.a.
National Science Foundation (Hrsg.)
Washington, D.C.: U.S. Government Printing Office 1978. XII, 229 S.
Bibl.; Anm.; Tab.

Children; Effects Research; Literature Reviews; Research Needs; Television Advertising; United States

63
Roberts, Donald F.
Children and commercials. Issues, evidence, interventions.
In: Rx televison.
Sprafkin, Joyce (Hrsg.) u.a.

New York, N.Y.: Haworth 1983, S. 19-35.
Bibl.

Age Differences; Children; Effects Research; Literature Reviews; Practical
Relevance; Prevention; Television Advertising; United States

64
Saxer Ulrich; Bonfadelli, Heinz; Hättenschwiler, Walter
Die Massenmedien im Leben der Kinder und Jugendlichen. Eine Studie
zur Mediensozialisation im Spannungsfeld von Familie, Schule und
Kameraden.
Zug: Klett und Ballmer 1980. 275 S.
(Zürcher Beiträge zur Medienpädagogik.)
ISBN 3-264-90210-9
Bibl.; Anm.; Abb.; Tab.; Gph.

Adolescents; Children; Interviews; Mass Media; Media Uses; Recipient
Research; Socialization; Switzerland

65
Searle, Ann
Children's perception and understanding of television.
School of Behavioural and Social Science, Plymouth, Devon (Hrsg.)
Plymouth, Devon: School of Behavioural and Social Science, Plymouth
Polytechnic 1975. 18 S.
Bibl.

Children; Cognitive Development; Comprehension; Literature Reviews;
Perception; Television

66
Singer, Jerome L.; Singer, Dorothy G.
Implications of childhood television viewing for cognition, imagination,
and emotion.
In: Children's understanding of television.
Bryant, Jennings (Hrsg.) u.a.
New York, N.Y. u.a.: Academic Press 1983, S. 265-295.
Bibl.

Children; Cognition; Effects Research; Emotions; Imagery; Literature
Reviews; Parent Participation; Television

67
Singer, Jerome L.; Singer, Dorothy G.
Television, imagination, and aggression.
A study of preschoolers.
Hillsdale, N.J.: Erlbaum 1981. 213 S.
ISBN 0-89859-060-4
Bibl.; Reg. Tab.; Gph.

Aggressive Behavior; Cognitive Development; Effects Research; Emotional Development; Family; Imagery; Imagination; Longitudinal Studies; Parent Influence; Play; Preschool Children; Speech; Television; United States

68
Sturm, Hertha
Neue Medien – Programmausweitungen. Das Problem sind die Kinder.
In: Fernsehen und Bildung, 16/1982/1 – 3, S. 235 – 245.
Bibl.

Children; Cognition; Effects Research; Emotions; Heavy Viewer; Program Extension; Social Behavior; Television

69
Television advertising and children. Issues, research and findings.
Esserman, June F. (Hrsg.); Barenblatt, Lloyd (Mitarb.); Klapper, Hope Lunin (Mitarb.); Zuckerman, Paul (Mitarb.) u.a.
Child Research Service (Hrsg.)
New York, N.Y.: Child Research Service 1981. 141 S. (Arlington, Va.: ERIC ED 214 645.)
Bibl.; Tab.; Gph.

Children; Compilations; Effects Research; Television Advertising

70
Television and behavior. Ten years of scientific progress and implications for the eighties.
1. Summary report.
Pearl, David (Hrsg.); Bouthilet, Lorraine (Hrsg.); Lazar, Joyce (Hrsg.)
National Institute of Mental Health, Rockville, Md. (Hrsg.); United States, Department of Health and Human Services, Washington, D.C. (Hrsg.)
Rockville, Md.: National Inst. of Mental Health 1982. VIII, 94 S.
Bibl.

Children; Effects Research; Historic Development; Learning; Socialization; Television; United States

71
Television and behavior. Ten years of scientific progress and implications for the eighties.
2. Technical reviews.
Pearl, David (Hrsg.); Bouthilet, Lorraine (Hrsg.); Lazar Joyce (Hrsg.)
National Institute of Mental Health, Rockville, Md. (Hrsg.); United States, Department of Health and Human Services, Washington D.C. (Hrsg.)
Rockville, Md.: National Inst. of Mental Health 1982. X, 362 S.
Bibl.; Anm.; Tab.; Gph.

Affect; Aggressive Behavior; Children; Cognition; Compilations; Effects Research; Health Education; Social Attitudes; Social Behavior; Television; United States; Violent Content

72
Television and human behavior.
Comstock, George (Mitarb.); Chaffee, Steven (Mitarb.) Katzman, Natan (Mitarb.) u.a.
New York, N.Y.: Columbia University Press 1978. XVIII, 581 S.
Bibl.

Audience Structure; Behavior Change; Effects Research; Everyday Life; Literature Reviews; Recreational Activities; Research Needs; Social Behavior; Television; Uses and Gratifications; Viewing Behavior

73
Television as a teacher. A research monograph.
Coelho, George V. (Hrsg.)
National Institute of Mental Health, Rockville, Md. (Hrsg.); United States, Department of Health and Human Services, Washington, D.C. (Hrsg.)
Rockville, Md.: National Inst. of Mental Health 1981. VIII, 269 S.
Bibl.

Children; Compilations; Effects Research; Learning Processes; Mass Media Effects; Television; United States

74
Viewing children through television.
Kelly, Hope (Hrsg.); Gardner, Howard (Hrsg.)
London u.a.: Jossey-Bass 1981. 107 S.
(New directions for child development. 13)
ISBN 87589-803-3
Bibl.; Reg.; Tab.

Children; Cognitive Processes; Compilations; Effects Research; Media Literacy; Recipient Research; Research Design; Television

75
Vorschule im Fernsehen. Ergebnisse der wissenschaftlichen
Begleituntersuchung zur Vorschulserie Sesamstraße.
Berghaus, Margot (Mitarb.); Kob, Janpeter (Mitarb.); Marencic, Helga
(Mitarb.); u.a.
Hans-Bredow-Institut für Rundfunk und Fernsehen, Hamburg (Hrsg.)
Weinheim u.a.: Beltz 1978. 204 S.
(Veröffentlichung des Hans-Bredow-Instituts für Rundfunk und Fersehen
an der Universität Hamburg)
(Beltz Monograpien: Soziologie.)

Activation; Cognitive Abilities; Conflict Resolution; Federal Republic of Germany; Parent Influence; Preschool Education; Program Evaluation; "Sesame Street"; Sex Roles; Social Learning

76
Wie Kinder mit dem Fernsehen umgehen. Nutzen und Wirkung eines
Mediums.
Sturm, Hertha (Hrsg.); Brown, J. Ray (Hrsg.)
Stuttgart: Klett-Cotta 1979. 330 S.
ISBN 3-12-930610-2
Bibl.

Children; Compilations; Effects Research; Recipient Behavior; Television; Viewing Behavior

77
Wie verstehen Kinder Fernsehprogramme? Forschungsergebnisse zur
Wirkung formaler Gestaltungselemente des Fernsehens.
Meyer, Manfred (Hrsg.)
Internationales Zentralinstitut für das Jugend- und Bildungsfernsehen,
München (Hrsg.)
München u.a.: Saur 1984. 315 S.

(Internationales Zentralinstitut für das Jugend- und Bildungsfernsehen:
Schriftenreihe. 17)
ISBN 3-598-20757-3
Bibl.; Gph.; Tab.

Children; Compilations; Effects Research; Formal Features; Formative
Evaluation; Media Literacy; Recipient Research; Television

78
Winn, Marie
Die Droge im Wohnzimmer. (The plug-in drug, deutsch).
Reinbek: Rowohlt 1979. 316 S.
ISBN 3-498-07286-2
Anm.

Behavior Disorder; Children; Cognitive Develoment; Family Relations;
Introductory Literature; Mass Media Effects; Media Criticism;
Recreational Activities; Television; United States

79
Winn, Marie
The plug-in drug.
New York, N.Y.: Viking Press 1977. XII, 231 S.
ISBN 0-670-56160-6
Anm.

Behavior Disorder; Children; Cognitive Development; Family Relations;
Introductory Literature; Mass Media Effects; Media Criticism;
Recreational Activities; Television; United States

80
Wolf, Michelle A.; Hexamer, Anne; Meyer, Timothy P.
Research on children and television. A review of 1980.
Aus: Communication yearbook. 5.
Nimmo, Dan (Hrsg.)
New Brunswick, N.J. u.a.: Transaction Books 1982, S. 353 – 368.
Bibl.; Tab.

Children; Effects Research; Literature Reviews; Professional Criticism;
Television; United States

Part II: Reception Processes

Chapter 3: Attention

81
Anderson, Daniel R.
Active and passive processes in children's television viewing.
Paper presented at a symposium on children's processing of information from television, American Psychological Association annual meeting, New York, September, 1979.
American Psychological Association (Hrsg.)
New York, N.Y.: APA 1979. 10 S., Anh.
Bibl.; Gph.

Comprehensibility; Cue; Literature Reviews; Peers; Preschool Children; Television; United States; Viewing Behavior; Visual Attention

82
Anderson, Daniel R.; Field, Diane E.
Die Aufmerksamkeit des Kindes beim Fernsehen. Folgerungen für die Programmproduktion.
In: Wie verstehen Kinder Fernsehprogramme?
Meyer, Manfred (Hrsg.)
München u.a.: Saur 1984, S. 52 – 92.
Bibl.; Abb.; Gph.

Attention; Children; Cognitive Development; Formal Features; Literature Reviews; Program Realization; Reception Processes; Recipient Research; Research Needs; Television

83
Anderson, Daniel R.
Children's attention to television.
Paper presented at the Biennial Meeting of the Society for Research in Child Development, New Orleans, La., March 17 – 20, 1977.
Society for Research in Child Development (Hrsg.)
Amherst, Mass.: Univ. of Massachusetts 1977. 18 S.
(Arlington, Va.: ERIC ED 136 958.)
Bibl.; Gph.

Attention; Children; Distraction; Effects Research; Television; United States; Visual Attention

84
Anderson, Daniel R.; Field, Diane E.
Children's attention to television. Implications for production.
In: Children and the formal features of television.
Meyer, Manfred (Hrsg.)
München u.a.: Saur 1983, S. 56 – 96.
Bibl.; Abb.; Gph.

*Attention; Children; Cognitive Development; Formal Features; Literature
Review; Program Realization; Reception Processes; Recipient Research;
Research Needs; Television*

85
Anderson, Daniel R.; Lorch, Elizabeth Pugzles
Looking at television: Action or reaction?
In: Children's understanding of television.
Bryant, Jennings (Hrsg.) u.a.
New York, N.Y. u.a.: Academic Press 1983, S. 1 – 33.
Bibl.; Tab.; Gph.

*Activity; Age Differences; Children; Comprehension; Cue; Literature
Reviews; Reception Processes; Recipient Research; Television; Theory
Formulation; United States; Visual Attention*

86
Anderson, Daniel R.; Lorch, Elizabeth Pugzles
A theory of the active nature of young children's television viewing.
Paper presented at the Biennial Meeting of the Society for Research in
Child Development, San Francisco, Calif., March 15 – 18, 1979.
Society for Research in Child Development (Hrsg.)
San Francisco, Calif.: Society for Research in Child Development 1979.
18 S. (Arlington Va.: ERIC ED 176 848.)
Bibl.; Gph.

*Comprehension; Cue; Expectation; Formal Features; Preschool Children;
Television; Theory Formulation; United States; Visual Attention*

87
Anderson, Daniel, R.; Levin, Stephen R.
Young children's attention to 'Sesame Street'.
In: Child Development, 47/1976/3, S. 806 – 811.
Bibl.; Anm.; Tab.; Gph.

*Age Differences; Attention; Effects Research; Formal Features; Infants;
Observation; "Sesame Street"; Sex Differences; United States*

88
Bryant, Jennings; Zillmann, Dolf; Brown, Dan
Entertainment features in children's educational television. Effects on
attention and information acquisition.
In: Children's understanding of television.
Bryant, Jennings (Hrsg.) u.a.
New York, N.Y. u.a.: Academic Press 1983, S. 221 – 240.
Bibl.; Gph.

*Children's Television; Educational Television; Effects Research; Formal
Features; Humor; Information Processing; Literature Reviews; Music;
United States; Visual Attention*

89
Calvert, Sandra L.
The effects of televised preplays on children's attention and
comprehension.
Paper presented at the Biennial Meeting of the Society for Research in
Child Development, Detroit, Mich., April 21 – 24, 1983.
Society for Research in Child Development (Hrsg.)
Greensboro, N.C.: Univ. of North Carolina 1983. 17 S. (Arlington, Va.:
ERIC ED 292 161.)
Bibl.; Gph.

*Age Differences; Children; Comprehension; Cue; Effects Research;
Presentational Form; Prosocial Content; Television; United States; Visual
Attention*

90
Children's understanding of television. Research on attention and
comprehension.
Bryant, Jennings (Hrsg.); Anderson, Daniel R. (Hrsg.)
New York, N.Y.: Academic Press 1983. XIV, 370 S.
ISBN 0-12-138160-9
Bibl.; Reg.; Tab.; Gph.

*Attention; Children; Compilations; Comprehension; Information
Processing; Media Literacy; Reception Processes; Recipient Research;
Television; Viewing Behavior*

91
The effects of action and violence in television programs on the social
behavior and imaginative play of preschool children.

Paper presented at the Meeting of the Southwestern Society for Research in Human Development, Dallas, Tex., March 1978.
Huston-Stein, Aletha (Mitarb.); Fox, Sandra (Mitarb.); Greer, Douglas (Mitarb.) u.a.
Southwestern Society for Research in Human Development (Hrsg.)
Dallas Tex.: Soc. f. Research in Human Development 1978. 15 S.
(Arlington, Va.: ERIC ED 184 524.)
Bibl.; Tab.

Arousal; Effects Research; Formal Features; Laboratory Experiments; Play; Preschool Children; Social Behavior; Television; Violent Content; Visual Attention

92
The effects of selective attention to television forms on children's comprehension content.
Paper presented at the Biennial Meeting of the Society for Research in Child Development, Boston, Mass., April, 1981.
Calvert, Sandra L. (Mitarb.); Huston, Aletha C. (Mitarb.); Watkins, Bruce A. (Mitarb.) u.a.
Society for Research in Child Development (Hrsg.)
Boston, Mass.: Society for Research in Child Development 1981. 10 S.
(Arlington, Va.: ERIC ED 224 605.)
Tab.; Gph.

Age Differences; Attention; Children; Comprehension; Formal Features; Laboratory Experiments; Television; United States

93
The effects of television commercial form and commercial placement on children's social behavior and attention.
Greer, Douglas (Mitarb.); Potts, Richard (Mitarb.); Wright, John C. (Mitarb.) u.a.
In: Child Development, 53/1982/-, S. 611 – 619.
Bibl.; Tab.; Gph.

Activation; Advertising; Aggressive Behavior; Formal Features; Laboratory Experiments; Play; Preschool Children; Television; Television Program Pacing; United States; Visual Attention; Visual Presentation

94
The effects of TV action and violence on children's social behavior.
Huston-Stein, Aletha (Mitarb.); Fox, Sandra (Mitarb.); Greer, Douglas (Mitarb.); u.a.

In: The Journal of Genetic Psychology, 138/1981/-, S. 183 – 191.
Bibl.; Tab.

Arousal; Children; Effects Research; Laboratory Experiments; Social Behavior; United States; Violent Content; Visual Attention

95
The effects of TV program comprehensibility on preschool children's visual attention to television.
Anderson, Daniel R. (Mitarb.); Lorch, Elizabeth Pugzles (Mitarb.); Field, Diane Erickson (Mitarb.) u.a.
In: Child Development, -/1981/52, S. 151 – 157.
Bibl.; Tab.

Attention; Comprehensibility; Laboratory Experiments; Preschool Children; Presentational Form; "Sesame Street"; United States; Visual Perception

96
Husson, William G.; Krull, Robert
Nonstationarity in children's attention to television.
In: Communication yearbook. 7.
Bostrom, Robert N. (Hrsg.) u.a.
Beverly Hills, Calif. u.a.: Sage 1983, S. 304 – 314.
Bibl.; Tab.

Age Differences; Attention; Children; Observation; "Sesame Street"; Television; United States

97
Husson, William G.
Theoretical issues in the study of children's attention to television.
In: Communication Research, 9/1982/3, S. 323 – 351.
Bibl.

Attention; Children; Professional Criticism; Television

98
Huston, Aletha C.; Wright, John C.; Potts, Richard
Fernsehspezifische Formen und kindliches Sozialverhalten.
In: Fernsehen und Bildung, 16/1982/1-3, S. 128 – 138.
Bibl.

Arousal; Attention; Children's Television; Effects Research; Formal Features; Observational Learning; Television; Violent Content

99
Huston-Stein, Aletha; Wright, John C.
Children and television. Effects of the medium, its content and its form.
In: Journal of Research and Development in Education, 13/1979/1,
S. 20 – 31.
Bibl.; Anm.

*Attention; Children; Comprehension; Effects Research; Formal Features;
Literature Reviews; Social Behavior; Television*

100
Huston-Stein, Aletha; Wright, John C.
Modeling the medium. Effects of formal properties of children's television
programs.
Paper presented at the Biennial Meeting of the Society for Research in
Child Development, New Orleans, Louisiana, March 17 – 20, 1977.
Society for Research in Child Development (Hrsg.)
Lawrence, Kan.: Univ. of Kansas 1977. 23 S.
(Arlington, Va.: ERIC ED 140 950.)
Bibl.; Tab.

*Age Differences; Arousal; Attention; Children; Comprehension; Effects
Research; Formal Features; Habituation; Learning Processes; Social
Behavior; Television; United States*

101
Krull, Robert
Children learning to watch television.
In: Children's understanding of television.
Bryant, Jennings (Hrsg.) u.a.
New York, N.Y. u.a.: Academic Press 1983, S. 103 – 123.
Bibl.; Tab.

*Attention; Children; Literature Reviews; Program Formats; Reception
Processes; Television*

102
Krull, Robert; Husson, William G.
Children's anticipatory attention to the TV screen.
In: Journal of Broadcasting, 24/1980/1, S. 35 – 47.
Anm.; Tab.

*Attention; Children; Effects Research; Laboratory Experiments; United
States*

103
Krull, Robert; Husson, William G.
Children's attention. The case of TV viewing.
In: Children communicating.
Wartella, Ellen (Hrsg.)
Beverly Hills, Calif. u.a.: Sage 1979, S. 83 – 114.
ISBN 0-8039-1171-8; 0-8039-1172-6
Bibl.; Tab.; Gph.

Attention; Children; Literature Reviews; Perceptional Development;
Recipient Behavior; Selective Perception; Television; Theory Formulation

104
Krull, Robert; Husson, William G.
Children's attention to the television screen. A time series analysis.
Paper presented at the Annual Meeting of the Association for Education
in Journalism, 60th, Madison, Wisconsin, August 21 – 24, 1977.
Association for Education in Journalism (Hrsg.)
Madison, Wis.: Association for Education in Journalism, Theory and
Methodology Division 1977. 47 S. (Arlington, Va.: ERIC ED 147 842.)
Bibl.; Gph.

Age Differences; Audiovisual Presentation; Children; Complexity; Effects
Research; Laboratory Experiments; Television; United States; Visual
Attention

105
Krull, Robert; Husson, William G.; Paulson, Albert S.
Cycles in children's attention to the television screen.
In: Communication yearbook. 2.
Ruben, Brent (Hrsg.)
New Brunswick N.J.: Transaction Books 1978, S. 125 – 140.
Bibl.

Age Differences; Attention; Children; Complexity; Effects Research;
Laboratory Experiments; Reception Processes; "Sesame Street";
Television; United States

106
Levin, Stephen R.; Anderson, Daniel R.
The development of attention.
In: Journal of Communication; 26/1976/2, S. 126 – 135.
Bibl.; Abb.; Gph.

*Attention; Effects Research; Infants; Laboratory Experiments; Program
Contents; Recipient Behavior; "Sesame Street"; United States*

107
Lorch, Elizabeth Pugzles; Anderson, Daniel R.; Levin, Stephen R.
The relationship of visual attention to children's comprehension of
television.
In: Child Development, 50/1979/-, S. 722 – 727.
Bibl.; Tab.

*Children; Comprehensibility; Comprehension; Distraction; Effects
Research; Laboratory Experiments; "Sesame Street"; Television; Toys;
United States; Visual Attention*

108
Mielke, Keith W.
Formative research on appeal and comprehension in '3-2-1 Contact'.
In: Children's understanding of television.
Bryant, Jennings (Hrsg.) u.a.
New York, N.Y. u.a.: Academic Press 1983, S. 241 – 263.
Bibl.

*Appeal; Attention; Children; Formative Evaluation; Program Series;
Recipient Behavior; Research Methodolgy*

109
Mock, Karen R.
Children's attention to television. The effects of audio-visual attention
factors on children's television viewing strategies.
Paper presented at the American Educational Research Association
Meeting, San Francisco, Calif., April 19 – 23, 1976.
University of Toronto, Canada, Faculty of Education (Hrsg.)
o.O.: o. Verl. 1976. 12 S. (Arlington, Va.: ERIC ED 122 832.)
Bibl.

*Auditory Attention; Canada; Children; Effects Research; Eye Movement;
Formal Features; Presentational Form; Television; Visual Attention*

110
Monkey Bars. Research report.
O'Bryan, Kenneth G. (Mitarb.); Maurizi, Maxene Raices (Mitarb.);
Zuckernick, Arlene (Mitarb.) u.a.
Ontario Educational Communications Authority, Toronto, Ontario,
Research and Development Branch (Hrsg.)
Toronto, Ontario: OECA 1974. 80 S.
(Papers and reports concerning educational communications. 46)
Tab.

*Age Differences; Audiovisual Presentation; Auditory Attention; Canada;
Children's Television; Comprehension; Cue; Laboratory Experiments;
Person Perception; Program Appreciation; Program Contents; Students;
Teachers; Television; Time Allocation; Viewing Behavior; Visual Attention*

111
Noble, Grant
Sesame Street and Playschool revisited.
In: Media Information Australia, -/1983/28, S. 27 – 32.
Bibl.; Tab.

*Attention; Australia; Children; Comparative Studies; Effects Research;
Participant Observation; "Sesame Street"; Viewing Behavior*

112
O'Bryan, Kenneth G.
Cues and attention to visual display in children's television.
O.O.: o. Verl. 1975. 11 S. (Arlington, Va.: ERIC ED 122 810.)

*Children's Television; Effects Research; Eye Movement; Learning
Processes; Presentational Form; Reception Processes; Summative
Evaluation; Television; United States; Visual Attention*

113
Pace and continuity of television programs.
Effects on children's attention and comprehension.
Wright, John C. (Mitarb.); Huston, Aletha C. (Mitarb.); Ross, Rhonda P.
(Mitarb.) u.a.
In: Developmental Psychology, 20/1984/4, S. 653 – 666.
Bibl.; Tab.; Gph.

*Age Differences; Attention; Children; Effects Research; Formal Features;
Retention; Television; Television Program Pacing; United States*

114
Pezdek, Kathy; Hartmann, Eileen F.
Children's television viewing. Attention and comprehension of auditory
versus visual information.
In: Child Development, 54/1983/4, S. 1015 – 1023.
Bibl.

Attention; Children; Cognitive Processes; Comprehension; Distraction;
Laboratory Experiments; Presentational Form; Reception Processes;
"Sesame Street"; Television; United States

115
Preschool children's visual attention to attributes of television.
Alwitt, Linda F. (Mitarb.); Anderson, Daniel R. (Mitarb.); Lorch,
Elizabeth Pugzles (Mitarb.) u.a.
In: Human Communication Research, 7/1980/1, S. 52 – 67.
Bibl.; Tab.

Attention; Audiovisual Presentation; Children's Television; Effects
Research; Laboratory Experiments; Preschool Children; Presentational
Form; Television; United States; Visual Perception

116
The relation between selective attention to television forms and children's
comprehension of content.
Calvert, Sandra L. (Mitarb.); Huston, Aletha C. (Mitarb.); Watkins,
Bruce A. (Mitarb.) u.a.
In: Child Development, 53/1982/-, S. 601 – 610.
Bibl.; Tab.; Gph.

Children; Comprehension; Formal Features; Observation; Retention;
Selective Perception; Television; United States; Visual Attention

117
Rice, Mabel L.; Huston, Aletha C.; Wright, John C.
Fernsehspezifische Formen und ihr Einfluß auf Aufmerksamkeit,
Verständnis und Sozialverhalten der Kinder.
In: Wie verstehen Kinder Fernsehprogramme?
Meyer, Manfred (Hrsg.)
München u.a.: Saur 1984, S. 17 – 51.
Bibl.; Gph.

Attention; Children; Comprehension; Effects Research; Formal Features;
Literature Reviews; Social Behavior; Television

118
Rice, Mabel L.; Huston, Aletha C.; Wright, John C.
The forms of television. Effects on children's attention, comprehension, and social behavior.
In: Television and behavior. 2.
Pearl, David (Hrsg.) u.a.
Rockville, Md.: National Institute of Mental Health 1982, S. 24 – 38.
In: Mass communication review yearbook. 4.
Wartella, Ellen (Hrsg.) u.a.
Beverly Hills, Calif. u.a.: Sage 1983, S. 37 – 52.
Bibl.; Gph.

Attention; Children; Comprehension; Effects Research; Formal Features; Literature Review; Presentational Form; Social Behavior; Television

119
Rice, Mabel L.; Huston, Aletha C.; Wright, John C.
The forms of television. Effects on children's attention, comprehension, and social behavior.
In: Children and the formal features of television.
Meyer, Manfred (Hrsg.)
München u.a.: Saur 1983, S. 21 – 55.
Bibl.; Gph.

Attention; Children; Comprehension; Effects Research; Formal Features; Literature Reviews; Social Behavior; Television

120
Rust, Langbourne W.; Watkins, Thomas A.
Children's commercials. Creative development.
In: Journal of Advertising Research, 15/1975/5, S. 21 – 26.
Bibl.; Abb.; Gph.

Attention; Children; Effects Research; Presentational Form; Television Advertising

121
Shively, Joe E.; Hines, Brainard W.; Cagno, Dick
Visual attention and enthusiasm to children's television programs.
Paper presented at the Annual Meeting of the American Educational Research Association, Washington, D.C., April 1975.
American Educational Research Association (Hrsg.)

Washington, D.C.: AERA 1975, 35 S. (Arlington, Va.: ERIC ED
104 367.)
Tab.

*Children's Television; Effects Research; Formal Features; Preschool
Children; Presentational Form; Program Effectiveness; Television; United
States; Visual Attention*

122
Susman, Elizabeth J.
Visual and verbal attributes of television and selective attention in
preschool children.
In: Developmental Psychology, 14/1978/3, S. 565 – 566.
Bibl.

*Comprehension; Effects Research; Formal Features; Laboratory
Experiments; Preschool Children; Prosocial Content; Television; United
States*

123
Wakshlag, Jacob J.; Reitz, Raymond J.; Zillmann, Dolf
Selective exposure to and acquisition of information from educational
television programs as a function of appeal and tempo of background
music.
In: Journal of Educational Psychology, 74/1982/5, S. 666 – 677.
Bibl.; Tab.

*Attention; Children; Educational Television; Formal Features; Information
Processing; Laboratory Experiments; Music; United States*

124
Wartella, Ellen; Ettema, James S.
A cognitive developmental study of children's attention to television
commercials.
In: Communication Research, 1/1974/1, S. 69 – 88.
Bibl.; Tab.; Gph.

*Age Differences; Attention; Audiovisual Presentation; Children;
Complexity; Effects Research; Laboratory Experiments; Television
Advertising; United States*

125
Wartella, Ellen
Individual differences in children's responses to television advertising.
In: Children and the faces of television.
Palmer, Edward L. (Hrsg.) u.a.
New York u.a: Academic Press 1980, S. 307 – 322.
Bibl.

Attention; Children; Comprehension; Effects Research; Literature
Reviews; Recipient Attributes; Recipient Behavior; Television Advertising

126
Watching children watch television.
Anderson, Daniel R. (Mitarb.); Alwitt, Linda F. (Mitarb.); Lorch,
Elizabeth Pugzles (Mitarb.) u.a.
In: Attention and cognitive development.
Hale, Gordon (Hrsg.) u.a.
New York, N.Y. u.a.: Plenum Press 1985, S. 331 – 361.
Bibl.; Tab.; Gph.

Children; Literature Reviews; Televiewing Frequency; Television; Viewing
Situation; Visual Attention

127
Watt, James H.; Welch, Alicia J.
Effects of static and dynamic complexity on children's attention and recall
of televised instruction.
In: Children's understanding of television.
Bryant, Jennings (Hrsg.) u.a.
New York, N.Y. u.a.: Academic Press 1983, S. 69 – 102.
Bibl.; Tab.

Audiovisual Presentation; Children's Television; Complexity; Content
Analysis; Formal Features; Learning Processes; Recall; Recognition;
Television; United States; Visual Attention

128
Welch, Alicia J.; Watt, James H.
The influence of visual complexity on children's attention to and learning
from 'Sesame Street'.
Paper presented at the Annual Meeting of the Association for Education
in Journalism, 63rd, Boston, Mass., August 9 – 13, 1980.
Association for Education in Journalism (Hrsg.)

Boston, Mass.: AEJ 1980. 14 S. (Arlington, Va.: ERIC ED 191 034.)
Bibl.; Tab.

Complexity; Laboratory Experiments; Learning; Preschool Children;
Visual Attention; Visual Presentation; "Sesame Street"; United States

129
Welch, Alicia J.; Watt, James H.
Visual complexity and young children's learning from television.
In: Human Communication Research, 8/1982/2, S. 133 – 145.
Bibl.; Tab.; Gph.

Attention; Audiovisual Presentation; Complexity; Effects Research;
Laboratory Experiments; Learning Processes; Preschool Children; Recall;
Recognition; "Sesame Street"; United States

130
Wright, John C.; Huston, Aletha C.
A matter of form. Potentials of television for young viewers.
In: American Psychologist, -/1983/July, S. 835 – 843.
Bibl.; Anm.

Attention; Children; Comprehension; Coviewing Adult; Effects Research;
Formal Features; Presentational Form; Social Behavior; Television; United
States

131
Zuckerman, Paul; Ziegler, Mark; Stevenson, Harold W.
Children's viewing of television and recognition memory of commercials.
In: Child Development, 49/1978/-, S. 96 – 104.
Bibl.; Tab.; Gph.

Laboratory Experiments; Peers; Recall; Students; Television; Television
Advertising; United States; Viewing Behavior; Visual Attention

Chapter 4: Comprehension

132
Abel, John D.; Beninson, Maureen E.
Perceptions of TV program violence by children and mothers.
In: Journal of Broadcasting, 20/1976/3, S. 355 – 363.
Anm.; Tab.

*Children; Comprehension; Interviews; Mothers; Program Appreciation;
Television; United States; Violent Content*

133
Age-related aspects of comprehension and inference from a televised
dramatic narrative.
Collins, W. Andrew (Mitarb.); Wellman, Henry M. (Mitarb.); Keniston,
Allen H. (Mitarb.) u.a.
In: Child Development, 49/1978/-, S. 389 – 399.
Bibl.; Tab.

*Age Differences; Audiovisual Presentation; Complexity; Comprehension;
Information Processing; Laboratory Experiments; Students; Television;
United States*

134
Banker, Gail S.; Meringoff, Laurene
Without words – the meaning children derive from a nonverbal story.
Harvard University, Cambridge, Massachusetts, Graduate School of
Education (Hrsg.)
Cambridge, Mass.: Harvard Univ. 1982. 169 S. (Arlington, Va.: ERIC ED
224 037.)
(Technical report 26); (Harvard project zero.)
Abb.; Tab.

*Children; Comprehension; Effects Research; Presentational Form;
Retention; Television; United States; Visual Presentation*

135
Baron, Lois J.
What do children really see on televison?
Paper presented at the Annual Meeting of the American Educational
Research Association, Boston, Mass.; April 7 – 11, 1980.
American Educational Research Association (Hrsg.)

Boston, Mass.: AERA 1980. 24 S. (Arlington, Va.: ERIC ED 188 784.)
Bibl.; Tab.

Age Differences; Children; Interviews; Reality Perception; Television;
United States

136
Bearison, David J.; Bain, Jean M.; Daniele, Richard
Developmental changes in how children understand television.
In: Social Behavior and Personality, 10/1982/2, S. 133 – 144.
Bibl.; Tab.

Adolescents; Age Differences; Children; Cognitive Development;
Comprehension; Social Interaction; Social Perception; Television; United
States

137
Calvert, Sandra L.
The effects of televised preplays on children's attention and
comprehension.
Paper presented at the Biennial Meeting of the Society for Research in
Child Development, Detroit, Mich., April 21 – 24, 1983.
Society for Research in Child Development (Hrsg.)
Greensboro, N.C.: Univ. of North Carolina 1983. 17 S. (Arlington, Va.:
ERIC ED 292 161.)
Bibl.; Gph.

Age Differences; Children; Comprehension; Cue; Effects Research;
Presentational Form; Prosocial Content; Television; United States; Visual
Attention

138
Charlton, Michael; Neumann, Klaus
Fernsehen und die verborgenen Wünsche des Kindes. Inhaltsanalyse einer
Kinderserie und Untersuchung des Rezeptionsprozesses.
Weinheim u.a.: Beltz 1982. 141 S.
(Beltz-Forschungsberichte.)
ISBN 3-407-58160-2
Bibl.; Abb.; Tab.; Gph.

Case Studies; Children; Children's Television; Content Analysis; Federal
Republic of Germany; Field Studies; Imitation; Kindergartens; Puppets;
Reception Processes; Summative Evaluation; Television; Uses and
Gratifications

139
Children's television commercials containing nutritional information.
When do they help? When do they hinder?
Paper presented at the Biennial Meeting of the Southwestern Society for
Research in Human Development, Lawrence, Kan., March 27 – 29, 1980.
Ross, Rhonda P. (Mitarb.); Campbell, Toni A. (Mitarb.); Wright, John
C. (Mitarb.) u.a.
Southwestern Society for Research in Human Development (Hrsg.)
Lawrence, Kan.: Society for Research in Human Development 1980. 8 S.
(Arlington, Va.: ERIC ED 190 211.)
Tab.; Gph.

Advertising; Attention; Children; Cognitive Development; Comprehension;
Expectation; Field Studies; Television; United States

140
Children's understanding of television. Research on attention and
comprehension.
Bryant, Jennings (Hrsg.); Anderson, Daniel R. (Hrsg.)
New York, N.Y.: Academic Press 1983. XIV, 370 S.
ISBN 0-12-138160-9
Bibl.; Reg.; Tab.; Gph.

Attention; Children; Compilations; Comprehension; Information
Processing; Media Literacy; Reception Processes; Recipient Research;
Television; United States; Viewing Behavior

141
Children's visual responses to Sesame Street.
Flagg, Barbara N. (Mitarb.); Allen, Bonita D. (Mitarb.); Geer, Abigail H.
(Mitarb.) u.a.
Center for Research in Children's Televison, Cambridge, Mass. (Hrsg.)
Cambridge, Mass.: Harvard Univ. 1976. 89 S. (Arlington, Va.: ERIC ED
212 378.)
Tab.

Children; Cognition; Comprehension; Eye Movement; Formative
Evaluation; "Sesame Street"; Testing; United States; Visual Attention

142
Collins, W. Andrew
Children's comprehension of television content.
In: Children communicating.

Wartella, Ellen (Hrsg.)
Beverly Hills, Calif. u.a.: Sage 1979, S. 21 – 52.
ISBN 0-8039-1172-6
Bibl.; Gph.

Age Differences; Children; Complexity; Comprehension; Literature Reviews; Perceptual Development; Reception Processes; Television; United States

143
Collins, W. Andrew
Children's processing of television content.
Implications for prevention of negative effects.
In: Rx television.
Sprafkin, Joyce (Hrsg.) u.a.
New York, N.Y.: Haworth 1983, S. 53 – 66.
Bibl.

Age Differences; Attention; Children; Cognitive Processes; Comprehension; Media Education; Television; United States

144
Collins, W. Andrew
The developing child as a viewer.
In: Journal of Communication, 25/1975/4, S. 35 – 44.
Bibl.; Abb.; Gph.

Age Differences; Children; Comprehension; Effects Research; Information Processing; Social Perception; Television; United States

145
Collins, W. Andrew; Sobol, Brian L.; Westby, Sally D.
Effects of adult commentary on children's comprehension and inferences about a televised aggressive portrayal.
In: Child Development, 52/1981/-, S. 158 – 163.
Bibl.; Tab.

Aggressive Behavior; Children; Comprehension; Coviewing Adult; Effects Research; Intervening Variable; Laboratory Experiments; Program Contents; Television; United States; Viewing Situation

146
Collins, W. Andrew
Interpretation and inference in children's television viewing.
In: Children's understanding of television.
Bryant, Jennings (Hrsg.) u.a.
New York, N.Y. u.a: Academic Press 1983, S. 125 – 150.
Bibl.; Gph.

Children; Cognitive Processes; Comprehension; Literature Reviews; Media Literacy; Person Perception; Reception Processes; Recipient Research; Retention; Social Understanding; Stereotype Portrayals; Television Advertising

147
Collins, W. Andrew
Schemata for understanding television.
In: Viewing children through television.
Kelly, Hope (Hrsg.) u.a.
London u.a.: Jossey-Bass 1981, S. 31 – 56.
Bibl.

Children; Cognitive Structure; Comprehension; Formal Features; Literature Reviews; Preconceptions; Reception Processes; Recipient Research; Television; United States

148
Collins, W. Andrew; Wellman, Henry M.
Social scripts and developmental patterns in comprehension of televised narratives.
In: Communication Research, 9/1982/3, S. 380 – 398.
Bibl.

Age Differences; Children; Comprehension; Laboratory Experiments; Reception Processes; Stereotype; Television; United States

149
Desmond, Roger Jon
Cognitive development and television comprehension.
In: Communication Research, 5/1978/2, S. 202 – 220.
Bibl.; Tab.

Children; Cognitive Development; Comprehension; Effects Research; Intervening Variable; Observation; Role Playing; Social Learning; Television; United States

150
Donohue, Thomas R.; Henke, Lucy L.; Donohue, William A.
Do kids know what TV commercials intend?
In: Journal of Advertising Research, 20/1980/5, S. 51 – 57.
Bibl.; Abb.; Tab.

Children; Cognitive Processes; Comprehension; Laboratory Experiments; Media Literacy; Television Advertising; United States

151
Drew, Dan G.; Reese, Stephen D.
Children's learning from a television newscast.
In: Journalism Quarterly, 61/1984/1, S. 83 – 88.
Anm.; Gph.

Children; Credibility; Effects Research; Learning; News; Presentational Form; Retention; Television; United States

152
Flagg, Barbara N.; Housen, Abigail; Lesser, Stella
Pre-reading and pre-science on Sesame Street.
Center for Research in Children's Television, Cambridge, Mass. (Hrsg.)
Cambridge, Mass.: Harvard Univ. 1978. 68 S. (Arlington, Va.: ERIC ED 212 379.)
Tab.

Comprehension; Effects Research; Eye Movements; Learning Processes; Preschool Children; Program Effectiveness; "Sesame Street"; Television Program Pacing; United States; Visual Attention

153
Friedlander, Bernard Z.; Wetstone, Harriet S.; Scott, Christopher S.
Suburban preschool children's comprehension of an age-appropriate informational television program.
In: Child Development, 45/1974/-, S. 561 – 565.
Bibl.; Gph.

Cognitive Abilities; Comprehension; Preschool Children; Reception Processes; Television; Television Program Pacing; Testing; United States

154
Huston-Stein, Aletha; Wright, John C.
Modeling the medium. Effects of formal properties of children's television programs.
Paper presented at the Biennial Meeting of the Society for Research in Child Development, New Orleans, Louisiana, March 17 – 20, 1977.
Society for Research in Child Development (Hrsg.)
Lawrence, Kan.: Univ. of Kansas 1977. 23 S. (Arlington, Va.: ERIC ED 140 950.)
Bibl.; Tab.

Age Differences; Arousal; Attention; Children; Comprehension; Effects Research; Formal Features; Habituation; Learning Processes; Social Behavior; Television; United States

155
Jalongo, Mary Renck
The preschool child's comprehension of television commercial disclaimers.
Paper presented at the Research Forum of the Annual Study Conference of the Association for Childhood Education International, April 14 – 7, 1983, Cleveland, Ohio.
Association for Childhood Education International (Hrsg.)
Cleveland, Ohio: ACEI 1983. 16 S. (Arlington, Va.: ERIC ED 229 122.)
Bibl.; Tab.

Advertising; Comprehension; Field Studies; Media Literacy; Preschool Children; Television; United States

156
Knowles, Ann; Nixon, Mary
Young children's understanding of emotional states as depicted by television cartoon characters.
In: Television and children: Comprehension of programs.
Kent, Sally (Hrsg.) u.a.
Clayton, Victoria: Monash Univ. 1983, S. 49 – 60.
Bibl.; Tab.

Animation; Australia; Children; Comprehension; Effects Research; Emotions; Laboratory Experiments; Reception Processes; Stereotype Portrayals; Television

157
Lorch, Elizabeth Pugzles; Anderson, Daniel R.; Levin, Stephen R.
The relationship of visual attention to children's comprehension of
television.
In: Child Development; 50/1979/-, S. 722 – 727.
Bibl.; Tab.

*Children; Comprehensibility; Comprehension; Distraction; Effects
Research; Laboratory Experiments; "Sesame Street"; Television; Toys;
United States; Visual Attention*

158
Meringoff, Laurene Krasny
Influence of the medium on children's story apprehension.
In: Journal of Educational Psychology, 72/1980/2, S. 240 – 249.
Bibl.; Tab.

*Books; Children; Comparative Analysis; Comprehension; Effects
Research; Laboratory Experiments; Presentational Form; Reception
Processes; Retention; Television; United States*

159
Newcomb, Andrew F.; Collins, W. Andrew
Children's comprehension of family role portrayals in televised dramas.
Effects of socioeconomic status, ethnicity, and age.
In: Developmental Psychology, 15/1979/4, S. 417 – 423.
Bibl.; Tab.

*Age Differences; Children; Comprehension; Effects Research; Family;
Laboratory Experiments; Program Contents; Racial Differences; Recipient
Attributes; Social Stratum; Stereotype Portrayals; Television; United
States*

160
Palmer, Edward L.; MacDowell, Cynthia N.
Children's understanding of nutritional information presented in breakfast
cereal commercials.
In: Journal of Broadcasting, 25/1981/3, S. 295 – 302.
Anm.; Tab.

*Auditory Presentation; Children; Comprehension; Effects Research; Food
Advertising; Nutrition Instruction; Survey; Television; United States;
Visual Presentation*

161
Pezdek, Kathy; Stevens, Ellen
Children's memory for auditory and visual information on television.
In: Developmental Psychology, 20/1984/-, S. 212 – 218.
Bibl.; Tab.

*Children; Cognitive Processes; Comparative Analysis; Laboratory
Experiments; Presentational Form; Retention; "Sesame Street"; United
States*

162
Pingree, Suzanne
Another look at children's comprehension of television.
Hawkins, Robert P. (Mitarb.); Rouner, Donna (Mitarb.); Burns, John
(Mitarb.) u.a.
In: Communication Research, 11/1984/4, S. 477 – 496.
Bibl.; Tab.

*Age Differences; Children; Complexity; Comprehension; Effects Research;
Laboratory Experiments; Television; United States*

163
Reid, Leonard N.; Frazer, Charles F.
Children's interactional experience with television advertising as an index
of viewing sophistication. A symbolic interactionist study.
Paper presented at the Annual Meeting of the Association for Education
in Journalism, 62nd, Houston, Tex., August 5 – 8, 1979.
Association for Education in Journalism (Hrsg.)
Houston, Tex.: AEJ 1979. 23 S. (Arlington, Va.: ERIC ED 174 996.)
Bibl.; Tab.

*Children; Comprehension; Participant Observation; Symbolic
Interactionism; Television Advertising; United States*

164
Reid, Leonard N.
The impact of family group interaction on children's understanding of
television advertising.
In: Journal of Advertising, 8/1979/3, S. 13 – 19.
Bibl.; Gph.

*Children; Comprehension; Effects Research; Family Relations; Interviews;
Participant Observation; Television Advertising; United States*

165
Rendell, Peter; Nixon, Mary
Children's comprehension of television programs.
In: Television and children: Comprehension of programs.
Kent, Sally (Hrsg.) u.a.
Clayton, Victoria: Monash Univ. 1983, S. 1 – 27.
Bibl.; Tab.; Gph.

Age Differences; Australia; Children; Effects Research; Laboratory
Experiments; Recall; Reception Processes; Recognition; Television

166
Rendell, Peter; Nixon, Mary
Development of children's comprehension of television.
In: Media Information Australia, -/1980/18, S. 29 – 33.
Bibl.; Tab.; Gph.

Children; Comprehension; Reception Processes; Research Methodology;
Retention; Television

167
Rice, Mabel L.; Huston, Aletha C.; Wright, John C.
Fernsehspezifische Formen und ihr Einfluß auf Aufmerksamkeit,
Verständnis und Sozialverhalten der Kinder.
In: Wie verstehen Kinder Fernsehprogramme?
Meyer, Manfred (Hrsg.)
München u.a.: Saur 1984, S. 17 – 51.
Bibl.; Gph.

Attention; Children; Comprehension; Effects Research; Formal Features;
Literature Reviews; Social Behavior; Television

168
Rice, Mabel L.; Huston, Aletha C.; Wright, John C.
The forms of television. Effects on children's attention, comprehension,
and social behavior.
In: Television and behavior. 2.
Pearl, David (Hrsg.) u.a.
Rockville, Md.: National Institute of Mental Health 1982, S. 24 – 38.
In: Mass communication review yearbook. 4.

Wartella, Ellen (Hrsg.) u.a.
Beverly Hills, Calif. u.a.: Sage 1983, S. 37 – 52.
Bibl.; Gph.

Attention; Children; Comprehension; Effects Research; Formal Features;
Literature Reviews; Presentational Form; Social Behavior; Television

169
Rice, Mabel L.; Huston, Aletha C.; Wright, John C.
The forms of television. Effects on children's attention, comprehension,
and social behavior.
In: Children and the formal features of television.
Meyer, Manfred (Hrsg.)
München u.a.: Saur 1983, S. 21 – 55.
Bibl.; Gph.

Attention; Children; Comprehension; Effects Research; Formal Features;
Literature Reviews; Social Behavior; Television

170
Rossiter, John R.; Robertson, Thomas S.
Canonical analysis of developmental, social, and experiential factors in
children's comprehension of television advertising.
In: Journal of Genetic Psychology, 129/1976/2, S. 317 – 327.
Bibl.; Anm.; Tab.

Age Differences; Attitudes; Children; Comprehension; Interviews;
Socialization; Television Advertising; United States

171
Rydin, Ingegerd
Children's understanding of television. Preschool children's perception of
an informative programme.
Swedish Broadcasting Corporation, Stockholm, Audience and Programme
Research Department (Hrsg.)
Stockholm: Swedish Broadcasting Corp. 1976. 36, V S.
Bibl.; Abb.

Age Differences; Comprehension; Information Processing; Preschool
Children; Reception Processes; Retention; Sweden; Television

172
Rydin, Ingegerd
Children's understanding of television.
2. From seed to telephone pole. With moving pictures or stills?
Swedish Broadcasting Corporation, Stockholm, Audience and Programme
Research Department (Hrsg.)
Stockholm: Swedish Broadcasting Corp. 1979. 70 S.
ISBN 91-7552-202-0
Bibl.; Abb.; Tab.; Gph.

*Animation; Auditory Presentation; Children; Comprehension; Effects
Research; Interviews; Laboratory Experiments; Presentational Form;
Sweden; Television; Visual Presentation*

173
Rydin, Ingegerd
How children understand television and learn from it. A Swedish
perspective.
In: Children and the formal features of television.
Meyer, Manfred (Hrsg.)
München u.a: Saur 1983, S. 166 – 187.
Bibl.

*Children; Cognitive Development; Comprehension; Effects Research;
Formal Features; Learning Processes; Literature Reviews; Sweden;
Television*

174
Rydin, Ingegerd
Wie Kinder Fernsehsendungen verstehen und daraus lernen.
In: Wie verstehen Kinder Fernsehprogramme?
Meyer, Manfred (Hrsg.)
München u.a.: Saur 1984, S. 158 – 177.
Bibl.

*Children; Cognitive Development; Comprehension; Effects Research;
Formal Features; Learning Processes; Literature Reviews; Sweden;
Television*

175
Smith, Robin
Preschool children's comprehension of television.
Paper presented at the Biennial Meeting of the Society for Research in
Child Development, Boston, Mass. April 2 – 5, 1981.

Society for Research in Child Development (Hrsg.)
Boston, Mass.: Society for Research in Child Development 1981. 16 S.
(Arlington, Va.: ERIC ED 204 024.)
Tab.; Gph.

*Age Differences; Audiovisual Presentation; Comprehension; Formal
Features; Laboratory Experiments; Preschool Children; Television; United
States*

176
Storm, Susan Ruotsala
Comprehension: The challenge for children's television. Report of a study
of children's comprehension of selected segments of commercially and
educationally broadcast television programs.
Paper presented at the Annual Meeting of the Association for Educational
Communications and Technology, Miami Beach, Fla., April 28, 1977.
Association for Educational Communications and Technology (Hrsg.)
Miami Beach, Fla.: Association for Educational Communications and
Technology 1977. 20 S. (Arlington, Va.: ERIC ED 142 197.)
Bibl.; Tab.

*Advertising; Children's Television; Comparative Studies; Laboratory
Experiments; News; Preschool Children; Television; United States*

177
Television and children: Comprehension of programs.
Kent, Sally (Hrsg.); Nixon, Mary (Mitarb.); Knowles, Ann (Mitarb.) u.a.
Monash University, Clayton, Victoria, Faculty of Education (Hrsg.)
Clayton, Victoria: Monash Univ. 1983. 77 S.
(Research monograph. 7)
Bibl.; Tab.; Gph.

*Australia; Children; Comprehension; Effects Research; Reception
Processes; Television*

178
Wartella, Ellen
The child as viewer.
In: Education for the television age.
Ploghoft, Milton E. (Hrsg.) u.a.
Springfield, Ill.: Thomas 1981, S. 28 – 34.
Bibl.

*Age Differences; Media Literacy; Preschool Children; Reception
Processes; Students; Television*

179
Wartella, Ellen
Children and television. The development of the child's understanding of
the medium.
In: Mass communication review yearbook. 1.
Wilhoit, G. Cleveland (Hrsg.) u.a.
Beverly Hills, Calif. u.a.: Sage 1980, S. 516–553.
ISBN 0-8039-1186-6
Bibl.; Anm.

*Attention; Children; Cognitive Development; Information Processing;
Literature Reviews; Reception Processes; Television; Television Advertising*

180
Wartella, Ellen; Hunter, Linda S.
Children and the formats of television advertising.
In: Children and the formal features of television.
Meyer, Manfred (Hrsg.)
München u.a.: Saur 1983, S. 144–165.
Bibl.

*Attention; Children; Comprehension; Effects Research; Formal Features;
Literature Reviews; Persuasive Communication; Presentational Form;
Recall; Reception Processes; Television Advertising*

181
Wartella, Ellen
Individual differences in children's responses to television advertising.
In: Children and the faces of television.
Palmer, Edward L. (Hrsg.) u.a.
New York, N.Y. u.a.: Academic Press 1980, S. 307–322.
Bibl.

*Attention; Children; Comprehension; Effects Research; Literature
Reviews; Recipient Attributes; Recipient Behavior; Television Advertising*

182
Wartella, Ellen; Hunter, Linda S.
Präsentationsformen der Fernsehwerbung und ihre Wirkung auf Kinder.
In: Wie verstehen Kinder Fernsehprogramme?

Meyer, Manfred (Hrsg.)
München u.a.: Saur 1984, S. 138 – 157.
Bibl.

Attention; Children; Comprehension; Effects Research; Formal Features;
Literature Reviews; Persuasive Communication; Presentational Form;
Recall; Reception Processes; Television Advertising

183
Wilder, Paula Gillen
The development of preschoolers' apprehension of a televised narrative.
Harvard University, Cambridge, Mass., Graduate School of Education
(Hrsg.)
Cambridge, Mass.: Harvard Univ. 1979. 20 S. (Arlington, Va.: ERIC ED
184 113.)
(Technical report. 12); (Harvard project zero.)
Gph.

Attention; Audiovisual Presentation; Case Studies; Complexity;
Comprehension; Information Processing; Longitudinal Studies; Person
Perception; Play; Preschool Children; "Sesame Street"; Stereotype;
Television Program Pacing; United States; Viewing Behavior

184
Wilder, Paula Gillen
The moral of a story. Preschoolers' gradual comprehension of a narrative
on Sesame Street.
In: Moral Education Forum, 5/1980/3, S. 2 – 14.
Gph.

Attention; Case Studies; Comprehension; Longitudinal Studies; Preschool
Children; "Sesame Street"; United States; Viewing Behavior

185
Wright, John C.; Huston, Aletha C.
Children's understanding of the forms of television.
In: Viewing children through television.
Kelly, Hope (Hrsg.) u.a.
London u.a.: Jossey-Bass 1981, S. 73 – 88.
Bibl.

Children; Cognitive Processes; Comprehension; Formal Features;
Literature Reviews; Media Literacy; Perceptual Development; Recipient
Research; Television; Viewing Behavior; Visual Attention

Chapter 5: Arousal and Emotions

186
Cantor, Joanne R.; Sparks, Glenn G.
Children's fear responses to mass media. Testing some Piagetian predictions.
In: Journal of Communication, 34/1984/2, S. 90 – 103.
Bibl.; Abb.; Tab.

Age Differences; Anxiety; Children; Effects Research; Piaget, J.; Questionnaires; Television; United States

187
Cantor, Joanne R.; Wilson, Barbara J.
Modifying fear responses to mass media in preschool and elementary school children.
In: Journal of Broadcasting, 28/1984/4, S. 431 – 443.
Anm.; Tab.

Anxiety; Children; Effects Research; Emotions; Identification; Laboratory Experiments; Presentational Form; Television; United States

188
Cohen, Akiba A.; Adoni, Hanna
Children's fear responses to real-life violence on television. The case of the 1973 Middle East War.
In: Communications, 6/1980/1, S. 81 – 93.
Bibl.

Anxiety; Children; Effects Research; Israel; Interviews; Laboratory Experiments; Observation; Television; Violent Content

189
Dorr, Aimée; Doubleday, Catherine; Kovaric, Peter
Emotions depicted on and stimulated by television programs.
In: Children and the formal features of television.
Meyer, Manfred (Hrsg.)
München u.a.: Saur 1983, S. 97 – 143.
Bibl.

Adolescents; Children; Emotional Development; Emotions; Formal Features; Literature Reviews; Program Contents; Recipient Behavior; Recipient Research; Television

190
Dorr, Aimée; Doubleday, Catherine; Kovaric, Peter
Im Fernsehen dargestellte und vom Fernsehen stimulierte Emotionen.
In: Wie verstehen Kinder Fernsehprogramme?
Meyer, Manfred (Hrsg.)
München u.a.: Saur 1984, S. 93 – 137.
Bibl.

Adolescents; Children; Emotional Development; Emotions; Formal
Features; Literature Reviews; Program Contents; Recipient Behavior;
Recipient Research; Television

191
Dorr, Aimée
Television and affective development and functioning: Maybe this decade.
In: Journal of Broadcasting, 25/1981/4, S. 335 – 345.
Anm.

Affect; Arousal; Children; Emotions; Empathy; Habituation; Literature
Reviews; Media Literacy; Needs; Reception Processes; Recipient Research;
Recognition; Television

192
Emotion und Erregung – Kinder als Fernsehzuschauer. Eine
psychophysiologische Untersuchung.
Sturm, Hertha (Mitarb.); Vitouch, Peter (Mitarb.); Bauer, Herbert
(Mitarb.) u.a.
In: Fernsehen und Bildung, 16/1982/1-3, S. 11 – 114.
Bibl.; Tab.; Abb.; Gph.

Arousal; Children; Effects Research; Emotion; Federal Republic of
Germany; Laboratory Experiments; Psychophysical Measurements;
Television

193
Lagerspetz, Kirsti M. J.; Wahlroos, Carita; Wendelin, Carola
Facial expressions of pre-school children while watching televised violence.
In: Scandinavian Journal of Psychology, 19/1978/3, S. 213 – 222.
Bibl.; Tab.

Arousal: Effects Research; Finland; Interviews; Miming; Participant
Observation; Preschool Children; Television; Viewing Behavior; Violent
Content

194
Palmer, Edward L.; Hockett, Anne B.; Dean, Walter W.
The television family and children's fright reactions.
In: Journal of Family Issues, 4/1983/2, S. 279 – 292.
Bibl.; Tab.

*Age Differences; Anxiety; Arsoual; Children; Effects Research; Program
Contents; Television; United States; Viewing Behavior*

195
Steinman, David R.; Sawin, Douglas B.
Moderators of boys' aggressive reactions to violence. Empathy and
interest.
Paper presented at the Meeting of the American Psychological
Association, 87th, New York, N.Y., September 1 – 5, 1979.
American Psychological Association (Hrsg.)
New York, N.Y.: APA 1979. 10 S. (Arlington, Va.: ERIC ED 178 206.)
Bibl.

*Age Differences; Arousal; Children; Effects Research; Emotions;
Empathy; Peers; Social Behavior; United States; Violent Content*

196
Sturm, Hertha
Les effets émotionnels de la télévision sur les enfants.
Aus: Les cahiers de l'animation, -/1977/15 – 16, S. 111 – 116.
Anm.

*Children; Comparative Analysis; Emotions; Federal Republic of Germany;
Longitudinal Studies; Radio; Reception Processes; Television*

197
Surbeck, Elaine; Endsley, Richard C.
Children's emotional reactions to TV violence. Effects of film character,
reassurance, age, and sex.
In: The Journal of Social Psychology, 109/1979/2, S. 269 – 281.
Bibl.

*Age Differences; Arousal; Children; Effects Research; Emotions;
Presentational Form; Puppets; Sex Differences; Television; United States;
Violent Content*

198
Wright, John C.; Huston-Stein, Aletha
The influences of formal features in children's television on attention and
social behavior.
Paper presented at the Symposium ,,Television and children: The medium
is unique in its form, not its content.'' Biennial Meeting of the Society for
Research in Child Development, San Francisco, Calif., March 1979.
Society for Research in Child Development (Hrsg.); Center for Research
on the Influences of Television on Children, Lawrence, Kan. (Hrsg.)
Lawrence, Kan: Univ. of Kansas 1979. 13 S. (Arlington, Va.: ERIC
ED 184 525.)

*Arousal; Attention; Effects Research; Formal Features; Preschool
Children; Role Models; Social Behavior; Television; United States*

199
Zillmann, Dolf; Hay, T. Alan; Bryant, Jennings
The effect of suspense and its resolution on the appreciation of dramatic
presentations.
In: Journal of Research in Personality, 9/1975/-, S. 307 – 323.
Bibl.

*Anxiety; Arousal; Children; Effects Research; Laboratory Experiments;
Presentational Form; Reception Processes; Television; United States;
Viewing Behaviour*

200
Zillmann, Dolf
Television viewing and arousal.
In: Television and behavior. 2.
Pearl, David (Hrsg.) u.a.
Rockville, Md.; National Institute of Mental Health 1982, S. 53 – 67.
Bibl.; Gph.

Arousal: Effects Research; Habituation; Literature Reviews; Television

Chapter 6: Cognition

201
Acker, Stephen R.; Tiemens, Robert K.
Children's perceptions of changes in size of televised images.
In: Human Communication Research, 7/1981/4, S. 340–346.
Bibl.; Gph.

Age Differences; Children; Cognitive Development; Laboratory Experiments; Reception Processes; Spatial Ability; Television; United States; Visual Presentation

202
Acker, Stephen R.
Speed, space, kids and the television cyclops. Viewers' perceptions of velocity and distance in televised events.
Paper presented at the Annual Meeting of the International Communication Association, Minneapolis, Minn., May 21–25, 1981.
International Communication Association (Hrsg.)
Honolulu, Hawaii: Univ. of Hawaii, Dept. of Communication 1981. 49 S.
(Arlington, Va.: ERIC ED 213 065.)
Bibl.; Tab; Gph.

Adolescents; Age Differences; Children; Effects Research; Piaget, J.; Spatial Ability; Television; United States; Velocity Perception

203
Acker, Stephen R.
Viewers' perceptions of velocity and distance in televised events.
In: Human Communication Research, 9/1983/4, S. 335–348.
Bibl.; Tab.

Adults; Children; Laboratory Experiments; Presentational Form; Television; United States; Velocity Perception

204
Anderson, Daniel R.; Smith, Robin
Young children's TV viewing. The problem of cognitive continuity.
University of Massachusetts, Amherst, Mass. Department of Psychology
(Hrsg.)

Amherst, Mass.: Univ. of Massachusetts o.J. (ca.1984). 48 S.
Bibl.; Gph.

Children; Cognitive Abilities; Cognitive Processes; Comprehension;
Formal Features; Literature Reviews; Television; Theoretical Criticism;
United States; Visual Attention

205
Cohen, Akiba A.; Salomon, Gavriel
Children's literate television viewing. Surprises and possible explanations.
In: Journal of Communication, 29/1979/3, S. 156–163.
Bibl.; Tab.; Abb.

Attention; Cognitive Development; Comparative Studies; Heavy Viewer;
Israel; Media Literacy; Ratings; Retention; Television; United States

206
Collins, W. Andrew; Westby, Sally Driscoll
Children's processing of social information from televised dramatic
programs.
Paper presented at the Biennial Meeting of the Society for Research in
Child Development, Denver, Colo., April 11, 1975.
Society for Research in Child Development, Denver, Colo. (Hrsg.)
O.O.: o.Verl. 1975. 12 S. (Arlington, Va.: ERIC ED 113 024.)

Age Differences; Children; Effects Research; Information Processing;
Laboratory Experiments; Reception Processes; Television; United States

207
Collins, W. Andrew
Cognitive processing in television viewing.
In: Television and behavior. 2.
Pearl, David (Hrsg.) u.a.
Rockville, Md.: National Institute of Mental Health 1982, S. 9–23.
In: Mass communication review yearbook. 4.
Wartella, Ellen (Hrsg.) u.a.
Beverly Hills, Calif. u.a.: Sage 1983, S. 195–209.
Bibl.

Age Differences; Attention; Children; Cognitive Processes;
Comprehension; Literature Reviews; Media Literacy; Reception Processes;
Recipient Research; Television

208
Collins, W. Andrew
Recent advances in research on cognitive processing television viewing.
In: Journal of Broadcasting, 24/1981/4, S. 327 – 334.
Anm.

Age Differences; Attention; Children; Cognitive Processes;
Comprehension; Literature Reviews; Media Literacy; Reception Processes;
Retention; Television

209
Corset, Pierre
La télévision rend-elle les enfants intelligents?
In: Les enfants et la télévision.
Hubert, Pauline (Hrsg.) u.a.
Bruxelles: RTBF 1985, S. 51 – 59.
Bibl.

Children; Cognitive Processes; Concept Formation; France; Learning;
Media Education; Reality Perception; Television

210
Gaines, Leslie; Esserman, June
A quantitative study of young children's comprehension of television
programs and commercials.
In: Television advertising and children.
Esserman, June F. (Hrsg.) u.a.
New York, N.Y.: Child Research Service 1981, S. 95 – 105. (Arlington,
Va.: ERIC ED 214 645.)
Bibl.; Tab.

Advertising; Age Differences; Children; Children's Television;
Comprehension; Interviews; Perceptual Discrimination; Television; United
States

211
Greenberg, Bradley S.; Reeves, Byron
Children and the perceived reality of television.
Paper presented at the Annual Meeting of the International
Communication Association, New Orleans, Louisiana, April 17 – 20, 1974.

International Communication Association (Hrsg.)
East Lansing, Mich.: Michigan State Univ., Dept. of Communication
1974. 34 S. (Arlington, Va.: ERIC ED 096 713.)
Bibl.; Tab.

*Children; Effects Research; Intervening Variable; Perceptual
Discrimination; Reality Perception; Reception Processes; Television;
United States*

212
Greenberg, Bradley S.; Reeves, Byron
Children and the perceived reality of television.
In: Journal of Social Issues, 32/1976/4, S. 86–97.
Bibl.; Tab.

*Children; Effects Research; Interpersonal Communication; Program
Contents; Reality Perception; Television; Testing; United States*

213
Hoijer, Birgitta; Rydin, Ingegerd
Études sur les programmes pour les enfants et sur les bulletins
d'information dans la perspective de la comprehension des individus.
In: Les sondages d'opinion. Études de radio-télévision. 29.
Bruxelles: RTBF 1981, S. 131–153.
Bibl.; Gph.

*Adults; Children's Television; Comprehension; Formal Features;
Information Processes; News; Preschool Children; Presentational Form;
Sweden*

214
Huston, Aletha C.; Wright, John C.
Children's processing of television. The informative functions of formal
features.
In: Children's understanding of television.
Bryant, Jennings (Hrsg.) u.a.
New York, N.Y. u.a.: Academic Press 1983, S. 35–68.
Bibl.; Tab.

*Attention; Children; Cognitive Processes; Comprehension; Effects
Research; Formal Features; Learning Processes; Literature Reviews;
Reception Processes; Television*

215
Jaglom, Leona M.; Gardner, Howard
Decoding the worlds of television.
In: Studies in Visual Communication, 7/1981/1, S. 33 – 47.
Bibl.; Tab.

*Case Studies; Classification; Cognitive Abilities; Longitudinal Studies;
Media Literacy; Person Perception; Preschool Children; Program
Formats; Reality Perception; Television; United States*

216
Jaglom, Leona M.; Fagre, Anitra; Wilder, Paula G.
Preschoolers' classification of the television world.
Harvard University, Cambridge, Mass., Graduate School of Education
(Hrsg.)
Cambridge, Mass.: Harvard Univ. 1980. 27 S.
(Arlington, Va.: ERIC ED 192 417.)
(Technical report. 16); (Harvard project zero.)
Tab.

*Age Differences; Case Studies; Longitudinal Studies; Perceptual
Discrimination; Preschool Children; Program Formats; Recipient
Research; Television; United States*

217
Klapper, Hope Lunin
Children's perceptions of television as a function of cognitive stage.
A preliminary inquiry.
Paper delivered at Annual Conference of American Association for Public
Opinion Research, Boltons Landing, New York, May 1974.
o.O.: o.Verl. 1974. 12 S.

*Children; Cognitive Development; Effects Research; Interviews; Piaget, J.;
Reception Processes; Television; United States*

218
Korzenny, Felipe
The perceived reality of television and aggressive predispositions among
children in Mexico.
Paper presented to the Instructional Communication Division at the
Annual Meeting of the International Communication Association,
Portland, Or., April 14 – 17, 1976.
International Communication Association (Hrsg.)

Portland, Or.: ICA 1976. 38 S. (Arlington, Va.: ERIC ED 122 336.)
Bibl.; Tab.

*Children; Mexico; Questionnaires; Reality Perception; Recipient
Attributes; Television; Violent Content*

219
Krendl, Kathy A.; Watkins, Bruce A.
Understanding television. An exploratory inquiry into the reconstruction
of narrative content.
In: Educational Communication and Technology, 31/1983/4, S. 201 – 212.
Bibl.; Tab.

*Children; Cognitive Processes; Effects Research; Laboratory Experiments;
Recall; Television; United States*

220
Kwiatek, Kathy Krendl; Watkins, Bruce A.
The systematic viewer. A developmental inquiry into the existence of a
television schema.
Paper presented at the Annual Meeting of the Association for Education
in Journalism, 65th, Athens, Ohio, July 25 – 28, 1982.
Tan, Zoe (Mitarb.)
Association for Education in Journalism (Hrsg.)
Athens, Ohio: AEJ 1982. 32 S. (Arlington, Va.: ERIC ED 218 633.)
Bibl.; Tab.

*Activity; Children; Cognitive Processes; Information Processing;
Interviews; Television; Testing; United States*

221
Levin, Stephen R.; Petros, Thomas V.; Petrella, Florence W.
Preschoolers' discrimination of television programming and commercials.
Paper presented at the Biennial Meeting of the Society for Research in
Child Development, San Francisco, Calif., March 15 – 18, 1979.
Society for Research in Child Development (Hrsg.)
Kent, Ohio: Kent State Univ., Dept. of Psychology 1979. 12 S.
(Arlington, Va.: ERIC ED 171 426.)
Bibl.; Gph.

*Advertising; Age Differences; Laboratory Experiments; Perceptual
Discrimination; Preschool Children; Program Formats; Television; United
States*

222
Meringoff, Laurene Krasny; Lesser, Gerald S.
Children's ability to distinguish television commercials from program material.
In: The effects of television advertising on children.
Adler, Richard P. (Hrsg.) u.a.
Lexington, Mass. u.a.: Lexington Books 1981, S. 29 – 42.
Anm.

Children; Literature Reviews; Perception; Perceptual Discrimination; Program Contents; Television; Television Commercials; United States

223
Pingree, Suzanne; Hawkins, Robert P.
What children do with television. Implications for communication research.
In: Progress in communication sciences. 3.
Dervin, Brenda (Hrsg.) u.a.
Norwood, N.J.: Ablex 1982, S. 225 – 244.
Bibl.

Attention; Children; Comprehension; Literature Reviews; Reception Processes; Research Design; Television; Uses and Gratifications

224
Resnik, Alan J.; Stern, Bruce L.; Alberty, Barbara
Integrating results from children's television advertising research.
In: Journal of Advertising, 8/1979/3, S. 3 – 12.
Bibl.; Abb.

Children; Cognitive Processes; Effects Research; Learning Processes; Literature Reviews; Models; Reception Processes; Television Advertising; Theory Development; United States; Viewing Behavior

225
Rice, Mabel; Wartella, Ellen
Television as a medium of communication. Implications for how to regard the child viewer.
In: Journal of Broadcasting, 24/1981/4, S. 365 – 372.
Anm.

Children; Decoding; Encoding; Information Processing; Presentational Form; Reception Processes; Television

226
Robertson, Thomas S.; Rossiter, John R.
Children and commercial persuasion. An attribution theory analysis.
In: Journal of Consumer Research, 1/1974/1, S. 13 – 20.
Bibl.; Anm.; Tab.

*Attribution; Children; Cognitive Processes; Comprehension; Interviews;
Persuasive Communication; Television Advertising; United States*

227
Rogge, Jan-Uwe
Objektive und subjektive Hintergründe der Medienrezeption.
In: Der Medienmarkt für Kinder in der Bundesrepublik.
Jensen, Klaus (Hrsg.) u.a.
Tübingen: Tübinger Vereinigung für Volkskunde 1980, S. 252 – 326.
Anm.

*Action Approach; Case Studies; Children; Cognitive Processes; Effects
Research; Federal Republic of Germany; Perception; Reception Processes;
Symbolic Interactionism; Television*

228
Rossiter, John R.; Robertson, Thomas S.
Children's TV commercials. Testing the defenses.
In: Journal of Communication, 24/1974/4, S. 137 – 144.
Bibl.; Tab.

*Age Differences; Attitude Formation; Children; Cognitive Processes;
Effects Research; Interviews; Media Literacy; Perceptual Discrimination;
Persuasive Communication; Television Advertising; United States*

229
Rovet, Joanne F.
Can audio-visual media teach children mental skills?
Paper presented at the American Educational Research Association
Annual Meeting, San Francisco, Calif., April 19 – 23, 1976.
O.O.: o.Verl. 1976. 15 S. (Arlington, Va.: ERIC ED 122 827.)

Audiovisual Media; Children; Cognitive Development; Television

230
Rydin, Ingegerd
Children's understanding of television.
2. From seed to telephone pole. With moving pictures or stills?
Swedish Broadcasting Corporation, Stockholm, Audience and Programme
Research Department (Hrsg.)
Stockholm: Swedish Broadcasting Corp. 1979. 70 S.
ISBN 91-7552-202-0
Bibl.; Abb.; Tab.; Gph.

*Animation; Auditory Presentation; Children; Comprehension; Effects
Research; Interviews; Laboratory Experiments; Presentational Form;
Sweden; Television; Visual Presentation*

231
Rydin, Ingegerd
Information processes in pre-school children.
2. The tale of the seed. Facts and irrelevant details in a TV-Programme
for children.
Swedish Broadcasting Corporation, Stockholm, Audience and Programme
Research Department (Hrsg.)
Stockholm: Swedish Broadcasting Corporation 1976. II, 34 S. 14 S. Anh.
Bibl.; Abb.; Tab.

*Age Differences; Audiovisual Presentation; Effects Research; Information
Processing; Laboratory Experiments; Preschool Children; Retention;
Sweden; Television*

232
Salomon, Gavriel
Beyond the formats of television. The effects of student preconceptions on
the experience of televiewing.
In: Children and the formal features of television.
Meyer, Manfred (Hrsg.)
München u.a.: Saur 1983, S. 209 – 229.
Bibl.; Gph.

*Children; Expectation; Formal Features; Practical Relevance; Reception
Processes; Recipient Research; Television; Theory Formulation*

233
Salomon, Gavriel
Der Einfluß von Vorverständnis und Rezeptionsschemata auf die
Fernsehwahrnehmung von Kindern.
In: Wie verstehen Kinder Fernsehprogramme?
Manfred, Meyer (Hrsg.)
München u.a.: Saur 1984, S. 199 – 218.
Bibl.; Gph.

*Children; Expectation; Formal Features; Practical Relevance; Reception
Processes; Recipient Research; Television; Theory Formulation*

234
Salomon, Gavriel
Interaction of media, cognition, and learning.
An exploration of how symbolic forms cultivate mental skills and affect
knowledge acquisition.
San Francisco, Calif. u.a.: Jossey-Bass 1979. XXV, 282 S.
(The Jossey-Bass social and behavioral science series.)
ISBN 0-87589-403-8
Bibl.; Reg.; Abb.; Tab.; Gph.

*Cognition; Film; Instructional Television; Knowledge Acquisition;
Learning; Mass Media Effects; "Sesame Street"; Symbol System;
Television*

235
Salomon, Gavriel
Introducing AIME. The assessment of children's mental involvement with
television.
In: Viewing children through television.
Kelly, Hope (Hrsg.) u.a.
London u.a.: Jossey-Bass 1981, S. 89 – 102.
Bibl.

*Attention; Children; Knowledge Gain; Media Literacy; Models; Reception
Processes; Recipient Research; Self Regulation; Television; Theory
Development*

236
Salomon, Gavriel
The language of media and the cultivation of mental skills. A report on
three years of research.
Spencer Foundation (Hrsg.)
Jerusalem: Hebrew Univ. of Jerusalem 1977. 132 S. (Arlington, Va.:
ERIC ED 145 808.)
Abb.; Bibl.; Tab.

*Children; Cognitive Abilities; Cognitive Processes; Comparative Studies;
Effects Research; Israel; Knowledge Acquisition; Laboratory Experiments;
Learning Processes; Television; Television Program Pacing; United States*

237
Salomon, Gavriel
Shape, not only content. How media symbols partake in the development
of abilities.
In: Children communicating.
Wartella, Ellen (Hrsg.)
Beverly Hills, Calif. u.a.: Sage 1979, S. 53 – 82.
ISBN 0-8039-1171-8; 0-8039-1172-6
Bibl.; Gph.

*Audiovisual Media; Children; Cognitive Development; Knowledge
Acquisition; Mass Media Effects; Presentational Form; Symbol System*

238
Salomon, Gavriel; Cohen, Akiba A.
Television formats, mastery of mental skills, and the acquisition of
knowledge.
In: Journal of Educational Psychology, 69/1977/5, S. 612 – 619.
Bibl.; Tab.

*Activity; Cognitive Abilities; Complexity; Formal Features; Israel;
Laboratory Experiments; Learning; Students; Television*

239
Salomon, Gavriel
Television watching and mental effort. A social psychological view.
In: Children's understanding of television.
Bryant, Jennings (Hrsg.) u.a.

New York, N.Y. u.a.: Academic Press 1983, S. 181 – 198.
Bibl.

Attention; Children; Learning Processes; Media Literacy; Reception Processes; Self Regulation; Television; Theory Formulation; Viewing Behavior

240
Singer, Jerome L.
The power and limitations of television. A cognitive-affective analysis.
In: The entertainment functions of television.
Tannenbaum, Percy (Hrsg.)
Hillsdale, N.J.: Erlbaum 1980, S. 31 – 65.
Bibl.

Affect; Attention; Cognitive Processes; Emotions; Encoding; Information Processing; Media Psychology; Memory; Reading; Reception Processes; Viewing Behavior

241
Soldow, Gary F.
The processing of information in the young consumer. The impact of cognitive developmental stage on television, radio and print advertising.
In: Journal of Advertising, 12/1983/3, S. 4 – 14.
Bibl.; Tab.

Advertising; Age Differences; Children; Cognitive Development; Comparative Studies; Information Processing; Laboratory Experiments; Piaget, J.; Printed Material; Radio; Television; United States

242
Sturm, Hertha
The application of Piaget's criteria to television programmes for children.
In: Information programmes for children 7 to 12 years old.
Werner, Peter (Hrsg.)
Geneva: European Broadcasting Union 1977, S. 12 – 19.
Abb.

Adolescents; Children; Effects Research; Information Processing; Piaget, J.

243
Sturm, Hertha; Jörg, Sabine
Information processing by young children.
Piaget's theory of intellectual development applied to radio and television.
Internationales Zentralinstitut für das Jugend- und Bildungsfernsehen,
München (Hrsg.)
München u.a.: Saur 1981. 91 S.
(Communication Research and Broadcasting. 4)
ISBN 3-598-20204-0
Bibl.; Tab.

Children; Effects Research; Information Processing; Laboratory
Experiments; Piaget, J.; Presentational Form; Radio; Switzerland;
Television

244
Sturm, Hertha; Jörg, Sabine
Informationsverarbeitung durch Kinder. Piagets Entwicklungstheorie auf
Hörfunk und Fernsehen angewandt. Eine empirische Studie zu Wirkungen
von Fernsehen und Hörfunk.
Internationales Zentralinstitut für das Jugend- und Bildungsfernsehen,
München (Hrsg.)
München u.a.: Saur 1980. 95 S.
(Internationales Zentralinstitut für das Jugend- und Bildungsfernsehen:
Schriftenreihe. 12)
ISBN 3-598-20752-2
Anm.; Tab.

Children; Effects Research; Information Processing; Laboratory
Experiments; Piaget, J.; Presentational Form; Radio; Switzerland;
Television

245
Stutts, Mary Ann; Vance, Donald; Hudleson, Sarah
Program-commercial separators in children's television. Do they help a
child tell the difference between Bugs Bunny and the Quik Rabbit?
In: Journal of Advertising, 10/1981/2, S. 16 – 25.
Bibl.; Tab.

Age Differences; Children; Cue; Effects Research; Perceptual
Discrimination; Program Formats; Television Advertising; United States

246
Vibbert, Martha M.; Meringoff, Laurene K.
Children's production and application of story imagery. A cross-medium investigation.
Harvard University, Cambridge, Mass., Grad. School of Education (Hrsg.)
Cambridge, Mass.: Harvard Univ. 1981. 66 S.
(Arlington, Va.: ERIC ED 210 682.)
(Technical report. 23); (Harvard project zero.)
Bibl.; Abb.

Audiovisual Presentation; Auditory Presentation; Comparative Studies; Comprehension; Person Perception; Students; United States; Verbal Presentation

247
Wackman, Daniel B.; Wartella, Ellen; Ward, Scott
Learning to be consumers. The role of the family.
In: Journal of Communication, 27/1977/1, S. 138 – 157.
Bibl.; Tab.

Children; Cognitive Abilities; Family; Information Processing; Intervening Variable; Recipient Behavior; Recipient Research; Socialization; Television Advertising; United States

248
Wackman, Daniel B.; Wartella, Ellen
A review of cognitive development theory and research and the implication for research on children's responses to television.
In: Communication Research, 4/1977/2, S. 203 – 224.
Bibl.; Anm.

Attention; Cognitive Development; Concept Formation; Encoding; Literature Reviews; Mass Media Effects; Perception; Research Needs

249
Ward, Scott; Wackman, Daniel B.
Children's information processing of television advertising.
In: New models for mass communication research.
Clarke, Peter (Hrsg.)
Beverly Hills: Sage 1973. S. 119 – 145.
Bibl.

Children; Information Processing; Television; Television Commercials

250
Wartella, Ellen
Children's perceptual unitizing of a televised behavior sequence.
Paper presented at the Annual Meeting of the Association for Education
in Journalism, 61st, Seattle, Washington, August 13 – 16, 1978.
Association for Education in Journalism (Hrsg.)
Columbus, Ohio: Ohio State Univ., Department of Communication 1978.
33 S. (Arlington, Va.: ERIC ED 166 694.)
Bibl.; Tab.

*Age Differences; Children; Cognitive Processes; Laboratory Experiments;
Reception Processes; Television; United States; Visual Perception*

251
Williams, Tannis MacBeth
Processes involved in children's learning from television. A review of
research.
In: Television as a teacher.
Coelho, George V. (Hrsg.)
Rockville, Md.: National Institute of Mental Health 1981, S. 93 – 134.
Bibl.

*Age Differences; Attention; Children's Television; Cognitive Processes;
Comprehension; Learning Processes; Literature Reviews; Reception
Processes; Retention; Television*

252
Wright, John C.; Watkins, Bruce A.; Huston-Stein, Aletha
Active versus passive television viewing. A model of the development of
television information processing by children.
Paper presented at the Annual Meeting of the American Psychological
Association, Toronto, August, 1978.
American Psychological Association (Hrsg.)
Lawrence, Kan.: Univ. of Kansas 1978. 20 S.
(Arlington, Va.: ERIC ED 184 521.)
Bibl.

*Children; Decoding; Encoding; Environmental Influences; Information
Seeking; Information Processing; Presentational Form; Reception
Processes; Television; Theory Formulation*

253
The young child as a consumer.
Wartella, Ellen (Mitarb.); Wackman, Daniel B. (Mitarb.) Ward, Scott
(Mitarb.) u.a.
In: Children communicating.
Wartella, Ellen (Hrsg.)
Beverly Hills, Calif. u.a.: Sage 1979, S. 251 – 279.
ISBN 0-8039-1171-8; 0-8039-1172-6
Bibl.; Gph.

Effects Research; Information Processing; Laboratory Experiments;
Preschool Children; Recipient Behavior; Television Commercials; United
States

254
Young viewers' troubling response to TV ads.
Current advertising techniques may be neither effective nor responsible for
use with children.
Bever, T.G. (Mitarb.); Smith, M.L. (Mitarb.); Bengen, B. (Mitarb.) u.a.
In: Harvard Business Review, 53/1975/6, S. 109 – 120.
Abb.; Gph.

Age Differences; Children; Information Processing; Interviews; Perceptual
Discrimination; Television Advertising; United States

Chapter 7: Fantasy and Reality

255
Brown, Mac H.; Skeen, Patsy; Osborn, D. Keith
Young children's perception of the reality of television.
In: Contemporary Education, 50/1979/3, S. 129 – 133.
Bibl.; Tab.

Age Differences; Children; Effects Research; Fiction; Reality; Reality Perception; Television; Testing; United States

256
Discrimintaion of television programs and commercials by preschool children. Young children can make the distinction.
Butter, Eliot J. (Mitarb.); Popovich, Paula M. (Mitarb.); Stackhouse, Robert H. (Mitarb.) u.a.
In: Journal of Advertising Research, 21/1981/2, S. 53 – 56.
Bibl.

Children's Television; Interviews; Media Literacy; Perceptual Discrimination; Primary School; Reception Processes; Television; Television Commercials; United States;

257
Dorr, Aimée
No shortcuts to judging reality.
In: Children's understanding of television.
Bryant, Jennings (Hrsg.) u.a.
New York, N.Y. u.a.: Academic Press 1983, S. 199 – 220.
Bibl.; Tab.

Age Differences; Children; Formal Features; Media Literacy; Reality Perception; Reception Processes; Recipient Research; Television; United States

258
Downs, A. Chris; Rogne, Carol J.; Hiney-Langseth, Deidre
The real-pretend distinction in children's judgments of televised events.
Paper presented at the Biennial Meeting of the Southwestern Society for Research in Human Development, Lawrence, Kansas, March, 1980.
Southwestern Society for Research in Human Development (Hrsg.)

Lawrence, Kan.: Society for Research in Human Development 1980. 9 S.
(Arlington, Va.: ERIC ED 195 349.)
Bibl.

Age Differences; Laboratory Experiments; Perceptual Discrimination;
Preschool Children; Presentational Form; Reality Perception; Television;
United States

259
Egan, Lola M.
Children's viewing patterns for television news.
In: Journalism Quarterly, 55/1978/2, S. 337 – 342.
Anm.; Tab.

Children; Interviews; News; Perceptual Discrimination; Television; United
States; Uses and Gratifications; Viewing Behavior

260
Feshbach, Seymour
Fantasy and children.
Paper presented at the Annual Meeting of the American Psychological
Association, Anaheim, Calif., August 26 – 30, 1983.
American Psychological Association (Hrsg.)
Anaheim, Calif.: APA 1983. 6 S. (Arlington, Va.: ERIC ED 248 029.)

Catharsis; Children; Fiction; Imagination; Introductory Literature; Mass
Media Effects; Perceptual Discrimination; Reality; Television

261
Feshbach, Seymour
The role of fantasy in the response to television.
In: The Journal of Social Issues, 32/1976/4, S. 71 – 85.
Bibl.; Anm.

Aggressive Behavior; Children; Effects Research, Imagination;
Multivariate Analysis; Recipient Behavior; United States

262
Greenberg, Bradley S.; Reeves, Byron
Children and the perceived reality of television.
Paper presented at the Annual Meeting of the International
Communication Association, New Orleans, Louisiana, April 17 – 20, 1974.
International Communication Association (Hrsg.)

East Lansing, Mich.: Michigan State Univ., Dept. of Communication
1974. 34 S. (Arlington, Va.: ERIC ED 096 713.)
Bibl.; Tab.

*Children; Effects Research; Intervening Variable; Perceptual
Discrimination; Reality Perception; Reception Processes; Television;
United States*

263
Greenberg, Bradley S.; Reeves, Byron
Children and the perceived reality of television.
In: Journal of Social Issues, 32/1976/4, S. 86–97.
Bibl.; Tab.

*Children; Effects Research; Interpersonal Communication; Program
Contents; Reality Perception; Television; Testing; United States*

264
Hawkins, Robert Parker
The dimensional structure of children's perceptions of television reality.
In: Communication Research, 4/1977/3, S. 299–320.
Bibl.; Anm.; Tab.

*Age Differences; Children; Expectation; Laboratory Experiments; Reality
Perception; Reception Processes; Television; United States*

265
Jaglom, Leona M.; Wilder, Paula G.; Fagre, Anitra
How preschoolers explore the relationship between television and the real
world.
Harvard University, Cambridge, Mass., Graduate School of Education
(Hrsg.)
Cambridge, Mass.: Harvard Univ. 1979. 23 S.
(Arlington, Va.: ERIC ED 182 746.)
(Technical report. 11); (Harvard project zero.)
Bibl.

*Case Studies; Longitudinal Studies; Perceptual Development; Perceptual
Discrimination; Preschool Children; Reality Perception; Television; United
States; Verbal Behavior*

266
Jaglom, Leona M.; Gardner, Howard
The preschool television viewer as anthropologist.

In: Viewing children through television.
Kelly, Hope (Hrsg.) u.a.
London u.a.: Jossey-Bass 1981, S. 9 – 30.
Bibl.; Tab.

Formal Features; Infants; Longitudinal Studies; Participant Observation; Perceptual Discrimination; Person Perception; Preschool Children; Program Preferences; Reality Perception; Reception Processes; Recipient Research; Social Perception; Television; United States

267
Kelly, Hope
Reasoning about realities. Children's evaluations of television and books.
In: Viewing children through television.
Kelly, Hope (Hrsg.) u.a.
London u.a.: Jossey-Bass 1981, S. 59 – 71.
Bibl.

Books; Children; Cognitive Processes; Comparative Studies; Fiction; Formal Features; Media Literacy; Participant Observation; Perceptual Discrimination; Reality; Reality Perception; Recipient Research; Television; United States

268
Klapper, Hope Lunin
Children's perceptions of the realism of televised fiction. New wine in old bottles.
In: Television advertising and children.
Esserman, June F. (Hrsg.) u.a.
New York, N.Y.: Child Research Service 1981, S. 55 – 82. (Arlington, Va.: ERIC ED 214 645.)
Bibl.; Tab.

Children; Effects Research; Fiction; Interviews; Perceptual Discrimination; Social Perception; Socialization; Television; United States

269
Levin, Stephen R.; Petros, Thomas V.; Petrella, Florence W.
Preschoolers' awareness of television advertising.
In: Child Development, 53/1982/4, S. 933 – 937.
Bibl.; Tab.

Advertising; Audiovisual Presentation; Auditory Presentation; Laboratory Experiment; Perceptual Discrimination; Preschool Children; Television; United States; Visual Presentation

270
Meringoff, Laurene Krasny
The reality of television fantasy – the fantasy of television reality: What does it mean to children?
Phantasie und Wirklichkeit im Fernsehprogramm für Kinder. Prix Jeunesse Seminar 30. Mai bis 2. Juni 1983, München.
Stiftung Prix Jeunesse (Hrsg.); Internationales Zentralinstitut für das Jugend- und Bildungsfernsehen, München (Hrsg.)
München: Stiftung Prix Jeunesse 1983. 12 S.

Books; Children; Fairy Tales; Fiction; Imagination; Reality; Reception Processes; Televison

271
Morison, Patricia; Gardner, Howard
Dragons and dinosaurs. The child's capacity to differentiate fantasy from reality.
In: Child Development, 49/1978/-, S. 642 – 648.
Bibl.; Tab.; Gph.

Children; Cognitive Development; Image: Laboratory Experiments; Perceptual Discrimination; Reality Perception; United States

272
Morison, Patricia; MacCarthy, Margaret; Gardner, Howard
Exploring the realities of television with children.
Harvard University, Cambridge, Mass. (Hrsg.)
Cambridge, Mass.: Harvard Univ. 1978. 16 S.
(Arlington, Va.: ERIC ED 165 804.)
(Harvard project zero.)
Bibl.; Tab.

Age Differences; Cognitive Abilities; Interviews; Media Literacy; Perceptual Discrimination; Reality Perception; Students; Television; United States

273
Morison, Patricia; MacCarthy, Margaret; Gardner, Howard
Exploring the realities of television with children.
In: Journal of Broadcasting, 23/1979/4, S. 453 – 463.
Bibl.; Tab.

Age Differences; Cognitive Abilities; Interviews; Media Literacy; Perceptual Discrimination; Reality Perception; Students; Television; United States

274
Morison, Patricia; Kelly, Hope; Gardner, Howard
Reasoning about the realities on television. A developmental study.
In: Journal of Broadcasting, 25/1981/3, S. 229–242.
Anm.; Tab.

Children; Communication Research; Fiction; Perceptual Discrimination;
Program Contents; Reality; Reality Perception; Reception Processes;
Survey; Television; United States

275
Palmer, Edward L.; MacDowell, Cynthia N.
Program commercial separators in children's television programming.
In: Journal of Communication, 29/1979/3, S. 197–201.
Bibl.; Tab.

Children; Effects Research; Insertion; Perceptual Discrimination;
Television Advertising; United States

276
Reeves, Byron
Children's perceived reality of television and the effects of pro- and anti-
social TV content and social behavior.
Paper presented at the Annual Meeting of the Association for Education
in Journalism, 60th, Madison, Wis., August 21–24, 1977.
Association for Education in Jounalism (Hrsg.)
Madison, Wis.: AEJ 1977. 24 S. (Arlington, Va.: ERIC ED 146 631.)
Bibl.; Tab.

Children; Effects Research; Interviews; Perceptual Discrimination;
Program Contents; Social Behavior; Television; United States

277
Reeves, Byron
Perceived TV reality as a predictor of children's social behavior.
In: Journalism Quarterly, 55/1978/4, S. 682–689, 695.
Anm.; Tab.

Children; Effects Research; Interviews; Program Contents; Prosocial
Behavior; Prosocial Content; Reality Perception; Television; United States

278
Sawin, Douglas B.
The fantasy-reality distinction in televised violence. Modifying influences
on children's aggression.
In: Journal of Research in Personality, 15/1981/-, S. 323 – 330.
Bibl.

Age Differences; Aggressive Behavior; Effects Research; Fiction;
Preschool Children; Presentational Form; Prosocial Behavior; Reality; Sex
Differences; Television; United States; Violent Content

279
Singer, Dorothy G.; Singer, Jerome L.
Television and the developing imagination of the child.
In: Journal of Broadcasting, 25/1981/4, S. 373 – 387.
Anm.

Children; Fiction; Imagery; Imagination; Literature Reviews; Media
Literacy; Parent Participation; Perceptual Discrimination; Reality; Reality
Perception; Reception Processes; Recipient Research

Chapter 8: Social Perception

280
Atkin, Charles; Greenberg, Bradley; MacDermott, Steven
Race and social role learning from television.
In: Conference on Telecommunications Policy Research, 6th Airlie House, 1978: Proceedings of the Sixth Annual Telecommunications Policy Research Conference.
Lexington, Mass. u.a.: Lexington Books 1979, S. 7 – 19.
Bibl.; Tab.

Adolescents; Attitude Formation; Effects Research; Person Perception; Race; Racial Differences; Recipient Behavior; Social Perception; Survey; Television; United States

281
Bearison, David J.; Bain, Jean M.; Daniele, Richard
Developmental changes in how children understand television.
In: Social Behavior and Personality, 10/1982/2, S. 133 – 144.
Bibl.; Tab.

Adolescents; Age Differences; Children; Cognitive Development; Television; United States

282
Chombart de Lauwe, Marie-José
L'interaction enfant-télévision.
In: Les enfants et la télévision.
Hubert, Pauline (Hrsg.) u.a.
Bruxelles: RTBF 1985, S. 61 – 85.
Bibl.; Tab.

Children; France; Identification; Models; Self Concept; Social Learning; Social Perception; Socializing Agent; Television

283
Collins, W. Andrew
Interpretation and inference in children's television viewing.
In: Children's understanding of television.
Bryant, Jennings (Hrsg.) u.a.
New York, N.Y. u.a.: Academic Press 1983, S. 125 – 150.
Bibl.; Gph.

Age Differences; Children; Cognitive Processes; Comprehension;
Literature Reviews; Media Literacy; Person Perception; Reception
Processes; Recipient Research; Retention; Social Perception; Television

284
Collins, W. Andrew
Temporal integration and children's understanding of social information
on television.
In: American Journal of Orthopsychiatry, 48/1978/2, S. 198 – 204.
Bibl.

Age Differences; Children; Cognitive Processes; Comprehension;
Literature Reviews; Person Perception; Retention; Social Perception;
Television

285
Collins, W. Andrew
Temporal integration and inferences about televised social behavior.
Paper presented an the Biennial Meeting of the Society for Research in
Child Development, New Orleans, Louisiana, March 17 – 20, 1977.
University of Minnesota, Institute of Child Development (Hrsg.)
o.O.: o.Verl. 1977. 12 S. (Arlington, Va.: ERIC ED 140 962.)
Gph.

Age Differences; Children; Comprehension; Information Processing;
Social Perception; Social Competence; Television; United States

286
Durkin, Kevin
Children's accounts of sex-role stereotypes in television.
In: Communication Research, 11/1984/3, S. 341 – 362.
Bibl.; Tab.

Children; Interviews; Sex Roles; Social Perception; Stereotype; Television;
United Kingdom

287
Feilitzen, Cecilia von; Linné, Olga
Children and identification in the mass communication process. A
summary of Scandinavian research and theoretical discussion.
Swedish Broadcasting Corporation, Stockholm, Audience and Programme
Research Department (Hrsg.)
Stockholm: Swedish Broadcasting Corporation, Audience and Programme
Research Department 1974. 39 S.
Bibl.

*Children; Effects Research; Identification; Literature Reviews; Mass
Media; Person Perception; Research Needs; Scandinavia; Television;
Theory Formulation*

288
Feilitzen, Cecilia von; Linné Olga
Identifying with television characters.
In: Journal of Communication, 25/1975/4, S. 51 – 55.
Bibl.; Abb.

*Children; Identification; Literature Reviews; Reception Processes;
Scandinavia*

289
Fernie, David E.
Ordinary and extraordinary people. Children's understanding of television
and real life models.
In: Viewing children through television.
Kelly, Hope (Hrsg.) u.a.
London u.a.: Jossey-Bass 1981, S. 47 – 58.
Bibl.

*Age Differences; Attribution; Children; Cognitive Processes;
Comprehension; Identification; Interviews; Media Literacy; Person
Perception; Recipient Research; United States*

290
Fernie, David E.
Who flies, who cries? Children's understanding of people from television
and real life.

Paper presented at the Annual Meeting of the American Psychological Association, 88th, Montreal, Canada, September 1 – 5, 1980.
American Psychological Association (Hrsg.)
Montreal, Canada: APA 1980. 10 S. (Arlington, Va.: ERIC ED 221 267.)

Age Differences; Children; Effects Research; Identification; Interviews; Person Perception; Reality Perception; Television; United States

291
Jaglom, Leona M.; Gardner, Howard
The preschool television viewer as anthropologist.
In: Viewing children through television.
Kelly, Hope (Hrsg.) u.a.
London u.a.: Jossey-Bass 1981, S. 9 – 30.
Bibl.; Tab.

Formal Features; Infants; Longitudinal Studies; Participant Observation; Perceptual Discrimination; Person Perception; Preschool Children; Program Preferences; Reality Perception; Reception Processes; Recipient Research; Social Perception; Television; United States

292
Kohli, Martin
Die Bedeutung der Rezeptionssituation für das Verständnis eines Fernsehfilms durch Kinder. Eine experimentelle Pilot-Studie.
In: Zeitschrift für Soziologie, 5/1976/1, S. 38 – 51.
Bibl.; Tab.

Children; Effects Research; Empathy; Federal Republic of Germany; Intervening Variable; Laboratory Experiments; Mothers; Peers; Television; Viewing Situation

293
Learning about the family from television.
Buerkel-Rothfuss, Nancy L. (Mitarb.); Greenberg, Bradley S. (Mitarb.); Atkin, Charles K. (Mitarb.) u.a.
In: Journal of Communication, 32/1982/3, S. 191 – 201.
Bibl.; Tab.

Attitude Formation; Children; Effects Research; Family; Parent Influence; Social Perception; Television; United States

294
Liebert, Robert M.; Sprafkin, Joyce N.
Impact of television on children's social development. A review of selected research on the socializing effects of television on children.
In: School Media Quarterly, 5/1977/3, S. 163 – 170.
Bibl.

Children; Effects Research; Introductory Literature; Learning Process; Observational Learning; Prosocial Behavior; Stereotype; Television

295
List, Judith A.; Collins, W. Andrew; Westby, Sally D.
Comprehension and inferences from traditional and nontraditional sex-role portrayals on television.
In: Child Development, 54/1983/6, S. 1579 – 1587.
Bibl.; Tab.

Children; Comprehension; Effect Research; Laboratory Experiments; Retention; Sex Roles; Social Perception; Stereotype; Television; United States

296
Newcomb, Andrew F.; Collins, W. Andrew
Children's comprehension of family role portrayals in televised dramas. Effects of socioeconomic status, ethnicity, and age.
In: Developmental Psychology, 15/1979/4, S. 417 – 423.
Bibl.; Tab.

Age Differences; Children; Comprehension; Effects Research; Family; Laboratory Experiments; Program Contents; Racial Differences; Recipient Attributes; Social Stratum; Stereotype Portrayals; Television; United States

297
Purdie, Sharon I.; Collins, W. Andrew; Westby, Sally D.
Children's processing of motive information in a televised portrayal.
Paper presented at the National Conference of the Association for Childhood Education International, St. Louis, Missouri, April 8 – 13, 1979.

Association for Childhood Education International (Hrsg.)
Minneapolis, Minn.; Minnesota Univ., Institute of Child Development
1979. 10. S. (Arlington, Va.: ERIC ED 172 955.)
Tab.; Gph.

Age Differences; Attribution; Children; Effects Research; Laboratory
Experiments; Social Learning; Television; United States; Violent Content

298
Quarfoth, Joanne M.
Children's understanding of the nature of television characters.
In: Journal of Communication, 29/1979/3, S. 210–218.
Bibl.; Tab.; Gph.

Animation; Children; Effects Research; Perceptual Development;
Perceptual Discrimination; Person Perception; Presentational Form;
Puppets; Role Models; Television; United States

299
Reeves, Byron; Faber, Ronald
Children's impressions of television characters.
In: Conference on Telecommunications Policy Research, 6th Airlie House,
1978; Proceedings of the Sixth Annual Telecommunications Policy
Research Conference.
Lexington, Mass. u.a.: Lexington Books 1979, S. 39–56.
Bibl.; Gph.

Children; Impression Formation; Literature Reviews; Person Perception;
Reception Processes; Stereotype; Television

300
Reeves, Byron; Greenberg, Bradley S.
Children's perceptions of television characters.
Paper presented at the Annual Meeting of the Association for Education
in Journalism, College Park, Maryland, August 1976.
Association for Education in Journalism (Hrsg.)
College Park, Md.: Association for Education in Journalism, Theory and
Methodology Div. 1976. 30 S. (Arlington, Va.: ERIC ED 124 986.)
Bibl.; Tab.

Children; Field Studies; Personality Traits; Stereotype Portrayals;
Television; United States

301
Reeves, Byron; Greenberg, Bradley S.
Children's perceptions of television characters.
In: Human Communication Research, 3/1977/2, S. 113 – 127.
Bibl.; Tab.

*Children; Field Studies; Personality Traits; Stereotype Portrayals;
Television; United States*

302
Reeves, Byron; Garramone, Gina
Children's person perception. The generalization from television people to
real people.
In: Human Communication Research, 8/1982/4, S. 317 – 326.
Bibl.; Tab.

*Children; Effects Research; Identification; Laboratory Experiments;
Person Perception; Reality Perception; Television; United States*

303
Reeves, Byron
Children's understanding of television people.
In: Children communicating.
Wartella, Ellen (Hrsg.)
Beverly Hills, Calif. u.a.: Sage 1979, S. 115 – 155.
ISBN 0-8039-1171-8; 0-8039-1172-6
Bibl.; Gph.

*Children; Identification; Impression Formation; Literature Reviews; Mass
Media Effects; Person Perception; Reception Processes; Television*

304
Reeves, Byron; Lometti, Guy E.
The dimensional structure of children's perceptions of television
characters. A replication.
In: Human Communication Research, 5/1979/3, S. 247 – 256.
Bibl.; Tab.

*Activity; Children; Cognitive Processes; Humor; Identification; Person
Perception; Reception Processes; Sex Differences; Television; United
States*

305
Reeves, Byron; Miller, M. Mark
A multidimensional measure of children's identification with television characters.
In: Journal of Broadcasting, 22/1978/1, S. 71 – 86.
Anm.; Tab.

Children; Identification; Interviews; Sex Differences; United States

306
Reeves, Byron; Garramone, Gina M.
Television's influence on children's encoding of person information.
In: Human Communication Research, 10/1983/2, S. 257 – 268.
Bibl.; Anm.; Gph.

Attitude Formation; Laboratory Experiments; Person Perception;
Reception Processes; Students; Television; United States

307
Robinson, Shari L.; Jaglom Leona M.; Wilder, Paula G.
The video parade. Children's understanding of characters in the preschool years.
Harvard University, Cambridge, Mass., Graduate School of Education (Hrsg.)
Cambridge, Mass.: Harvard Univ. 1980. 35 S.
(Arlington, Va.: ERIC ED 194 906.)
(Technical report. 19); (Harvard project zero.)
Bibl.; Tab.; Gph.

Age Differences; Case Studies; Longitudinal Studies; Person Perception;
Preschool Children; Recipient Research; Television; United States

308
Sawin, Douglas B.
Assessing empathy in children. A search for an elusive construct.
Paper presented at the Biennial Meeting of the Society for Research in Child Development, San Francisco, Calif., March 15-18, 1979.
Society for Research in Child Development (Hrsg.); University of Texas, Austin, Tex. (Hrsg.)
Austin, Tex.: Univ. of Texas 1979. 18 S. (Arlington, Va.: ERIC ED 168 711.)
Tab.

Children; Effects Research; Empathy; Intervening Variable; Media
Psychology; Social Behavior; Television; United States

309
Scholl, Kathleen
Four young children construct reality. Television watching in the home.
Research prepared at Indiana University.
O.O.: o. Verl. o.J. (ca.1979). 30 S. (Arlington, Va.: ERIC ED 216 355.)
Bibl.; Tab.

*Case Studies; Observation; Piaget, J.; Preschool Children; Reality
Perception; Reception Processes; Social Perception; Television; United
States*

310
Sedlak, Andrea J.
Understanding an actor's behaviors. Developmental differences in plan
interpretations.
Paper presented at the Biennial Meeting of the Society for Research in
Child Development, New Orleans, La., March 17 – 20, 1977.
Society for Research in Child Development (Hrsg.); University of North
Carolina, Chapel Hill, N.C., Department of Psychology (Hrsg.)
Chapel Hill, N.C.: Univ. of North Carolina 1977. 15 S. (Arlington, Va.:
ERIC ED 148 476.)
Bibl.; Tab.

*Adults; Age Differences; Children; Communication Research;
Comprehension; Reception Processes; Social Perception; United States*

311
Wartella, Ellen
Children's impressions of television families.
In: Conference on Telecommunications Policy Research, 6th Airlie House,
1978: Proceedings of the Sixth Annual Telecommunications Policy
Research Conference.
Lexington, Mass. u.a.: Lexington Books 1979, S. 57 – 72.
Bibl.; Tab.

*Children; Content Analysis; Effects Research; Family; Program
Appreciation; Program Contents; Role Perception; Social Role; Survey;
Television; United States*

Chapter 9: Media Literacy

312
Amey, Lorne J.
Visual literacy. Implications for the production of children's television programs.
School of Library Service, Halifax, Nova Scotia (Hrsg.)
Halifax, Nova Scotia: Dahlhousie Univ., School of Library Service 1976.
III, 55 S.
(School of Library Service, Halifax, Nova Scotia: Occasional papers series.)
Bibl.

Children's Television; Media Literacy; Practical Relevance; Television; Theory Comparison; United States; Visual Perception

313
Anderson, James A.
Receivership skills. An educational response.
In: Education for the television age.
Ploghoft, Milton E. (Hrsg.) u.a.
Springfield, Ill.: Thomas 1981. S. 19 – 27.
Bibl.

Introductory Literature; Media Literacy; Media Theory; Recipient Research

314
Anderson, James A.; Ploghoft, Milton E.
Receivership skills. The television experience.
In: Communication yearbook. 4.
Nimmo Dan (Hrsg.)
Brunswick. N.J.: Transaction Books 1980, S. 293 – 307.
Bibl.; Tab.

Cognitive Abilities; Educational Objectives; Evaluation; Longitudinal Studies; Media Education; Media Literacy; Students; Teacher Participation; Television; United States

315
Anderson, James A.
Television literacy and the critical viewer.
In: Children's understanding of television.
Bryant, Jennings (Hrsg.) u.a.
New York, N.Y. u.a.: Academic Press 1983, S. 297 – 330.
Bibl.; Anm.

Children; Educational Objectives; Media Education; Media Literacy;
Television; Theoretical Criticsm; United States

316
Anderson, James A.; Ploghoft, Milton E.
Television receivership skills. The new social literacy.
Paper presented at the Annual Meeting of the International
Communication Association, Berlin, West, May 29 – June 4, 1977.
International Communication Association (Hrsg.)
Berlin, West: ICA 1977. 23 S. (Arlington, Va.: ERIC ED 140 364.)
Bibl.

Aggressive Behavior; Children; Consumer Education; Curriculum
Development; Imitation; Literature Reviews; Media Literacy; Role Models;
Television; United States; Violent Content

317
Children's critical evaluation of television content.
Symposium presented at American Psychological Association. Annual
Meeting 1976.
Leifer, Aimée Dorr (Hrsg.); Graves, Sherryl Browne (Hrsg.); Gordon,
Neal J. (Hrsg.) u.a.
Center for Research in Children's Television, Cambridge, Mass. (Hrsg.);
Children's Television Workshop (Hrsg.); American Psychological
Association (Hrsg.)
Cambridge, Mass.: Harvard Univ. 1976. 57 S.
(Center for Research in Children's Television, Cambridge, Mass.: Report.)
Gph.

Adolescents; Adults; Children; Media Literacy; Perceptual Discrimination;
Project Descriptions; Television; United States

318
Corder-Bolz, Charles R.
Television literacy and critical television viewing skills.
In: Television and behavior. 2.
Pearl, David (Hrsg.) u.a.
Rockville, Md.: National Institute of Mental Health 1982, S. 91 – 101.
Bibl.

Children; Literature Reviews; Media Education; Media Literacy; Parent Participation; Recipient Research; Research Needs; Television

319
Finn, Peter
Developing critical television viewing skills.
In: The Educational Forum, -/1980/May, S. 473 – 482.
Bibl.

Children; Introductory Literature; Mass Media Effects; Media Literacy; Television

320
Forte, Michael
Cognitive processes for evaluating the credibility of television content.
Paper presented at the Annual Meeting of the American Psychological Association, Washington, D.C., September 5, 1976.
In: Children's critical evaluation of television content.
Leifer, Aimée Dorr (Hrsg.) u.a.
Cambridge, Mass.: Harvard Univ. 1976, 9 S.
Gph.

Adolescents; Adults; Age Differences; Children; Cognitive Processes; Credibility; Racial Differences; Sex Differences; Television; United States

321
Graves, Sherryl Browne
Content attended to in evaluating television's credibilty.
Paper presented at the Annual Meeting of the American Psychological Association, Washington, D.C., September 5, 1976.
In: Children's critical evaluation of television content.
Leifer, Aimée Dorr (Hrsg.) u.a.

Cambridge, Mass.: Harvard Univ. 1976, 9 S.
Gph.

Adolescents; Adults; Age Differences; Children; Credibility; Interviews; Media Literacy; Perceptual Discrimination; Reality; Television; United States

322
Leifer, Aimée Dorr
Factors which predict the credibility ascribed to television.
Paper presented at the Annual Meeting of the American Psychological Association, Washington, D.C., September 5, 1976.
In: Children's critical evaluation of television content.
Leifer, Aimée Dorr (Hrsg.) u.a.
Cambridge, Mass.: Harvard Univ. 1976, 15 S.
Gph.

Adolescents; Adults; Age Differences; Attitude Change; Children; Credibility; Media Literacy; Racial Differences; Television; United States

323
Lull, James
Social uses of television in family settings and a critique of receivership skills.
In: Education for the television age.
Ploghoft, Milton E. (Hrsg.) u.a.
Springfield. Ill.: Thomas 1981, S. 164 – 172.

Children; Family Relations; Mass Media Effects; Media Literacy; Professional Criticism; Recipient Behavior; Television

324
Phelps, Erin M.
Knowledge of the television industry and relevant first-hand experience.
Paper presented at the Annual Meeting of the American Psychological Association, Washington, D.C., September 5, 1976.
In: Children's critical evaluation of television content.
Leifer, Aimée Dorr (Hrsg.) u.a.
Cambridge, Mass.: Harvard Univ. 1976, 9 S.
Gph.

Adolescents; Adults; Age Differences; Children; Media Industry; Media Literacy; Television; United States

325
Ploghoft, Milton E.; Anderson, James A.
Teaching critical television viewing skills. An integrated approach.
Springfield. Ill.: Thomas 1982. IX, 192 S.
ISBN 0-398-04616-6
Bibl.; Reg.; Tab.

Children; Media Education; Media Literacy; Practical Relevance;
Television

326
Ploghoft, Milton E.
What is basic about critical receiver skills?
In: Education for the television age.
Ploghoft, Milton E. (Hrsg.) u.a.
Springfield, Ill.: Thomas 1981, S. 125 – 131.
Bibl.

Children; Curriculum Development; Media Education; Media Literacy;
Television; United States

327
Singer, Dorothy G.; Zuckerman, Diana M.; Singer, Jerome L.
Teaching elementary school children critical television viewing skills. An
evaluation.
In: Education for the television age.
Ploghoft, Milton E. (Hrsg.) u.a.
Springfield, Ill.: Thomas 1981, S. 71 – 81.
Bibl.

Children; Media Education; Media Literacy; Primary School; Project
Descriptions; Television; United States

328
Wolf, Michelle A.; Abelman, Robert; Hexamer, Anne
Children's understanding of television. Some methodological
considerations and a question-asking model for receivership skills.
Aus: Communication yearbook. 5.
Nimmo, Dan (Hrsg.)
New Brunswick, N.J. u.a.: Transaction Books 1982, S. 405 – 431.
Bibl.

Children; Literature Reviews; Media Literacy; Reception Processes;
Research Methodology; Television; Viewing Behavior

329
Wright, John C.; Huston, Aletha C.
The information processing demands of television and media literacy in young viewers.
Paper presented in a symposium entitled: Discourse, television, and comprehension, American Educational Research Association, New York, March, 1982.
Center for Research on the Influences of Television on Children (Hrsg.); University of Kansas, Lawrence, Kan., Department of Human Development (Hrsg.)
New York, N.Y.: American Educational Research Association 1982. 16 S. (Arlington, Va.: ERIC ED 227 840.)
Bibl.; Tab.; Gph.

Age Differences; Attention; Children; Comprehension; Information Processes; Laboratory Experiments; Preschool Children; Program Formats; Television; Television Program Pacing; United States

Part III: Viewing Situation

Chapter 10: Viewing Behavior

330
Augst, Gerhard; Fenner, M.L.; Kaul, E.
Kinder vor dem Bildschirm.
Gesamthochschule Siegen, Forschungsschwerpunkt Massenmedien und Kommunikation (Hrsg.)
Siegen: Gesamthochschule 1979. 56 S., 12 S. Anh.
(MuK.2)
Bibl.

Children; Family Relations; Federal Republic of Germany; Ratings; Survey; Television; Viewing Behaviour

331
Die Auswirkung von Szenen zum sozialen Lernen aus der Fernsehserie „Sesamstraße" auf Vorstellungsinhalte und Spielverhalten von Kindern.
Charlton, Michael (Mitarb.); Haugg, Rolf-Michael (Mitarb.); Carsten, Uwe (Mitarb.) u.a.
In: Zeitschrift für Sozialpsychologie, 6/1975/-, S. 348–359.
Bibl.; Anm.; Tab.; Gph.

Children; Effects Research; Federal Republic of Germany; Imagery; Imagination; Laboratory Experiments; Play; "Sesame Street"; Social Learning; Summative Evaluation

332
Baron, Lois J.
Interaction between television and child-related characteristics as demonstrated by eye movement research.
In: Educational Communication and Technology, 28/1980/4, S. 267–281.
Bibl.; Abb.; Tab.

Canada; Eye Movements; Laboratory Experiments; Reading Skills; Recipient Attributes; Students; Television; Television Program Pacing; Viewing Behavior

333
Brody, Gene H.; Stoneman, Zolinda
The influence of television viewing on family interactions. A contextualist
framework.
In: Journal of Family Issues, 4/1983/2, S. 329 – 348.
Bibl.; Abb.

*Family Relations; Recipient Attributes; Television; United States; Viewing
Behavior; Viewing Situation*

334
Charlton, Michael; Neumann, Klaus
Fernsehen und die verborgenen Wünsche des Kindes. Inhaltsanalyse einer
Kinderserie und Untersuchung des Rezeptionsprozesses.
Weinheim u.a.: Beltz 1982. 141 S.
(Beltz-Forschungsberichte.)
ISBN 3-407-58160-2
Bibl.; Abb.; Tab.; Gph.

*Case Studies; Children; Children's Television; Content Analysis; Federal
Republic of Germany; Field Studies; Imitation; Kindergartens; Puppets;
Reception Processes; Summative Evaluation; Television; Uses and
Gratifications*

335
Flagg, Barbara N.
Children and television. Effects of stimulus repetition on eye activity.
In: Eye movements and the higher psychological functions.
Senders, J.W. (Hrsg.) u.a.
Hillsdale, N.J.: Erlbaum 1978, S. 279 – 291.
Gph.

*Age Differences; Children; Effects Research; Eye Movements; Formal
Features; "Sesame Street"; Television; United States*

336
Frazer, Charles F.; Reid, Leonard N.
Children's interaction with commercials.
In: Symbolic Interaction, 2/1979/2, S. 79 – 98.
Bibl.

*Children; Participant Observation; Recipient Behavior; Social Interaction;
Television Advertising; United States; Viewing Behavior*

337
Hawkins, Robert P.; Pingree, Suzanne
Uniform messages and habitual viewing. Unnecessary assumptions in
social reality effects.
In: Human Communication Research, 7/1981/4, S. 291 – 301.
Bibl.; Tab.

*Australia; Children; Criminality; Effects Research; Expectation; Program
Contents; Program Preferences; Questionnaires; Social Attitudes;
Television; Viewing Behavior*

338
Hollenbeck, Albert R.; Slaby, Ronald G.
Infant visual and vocal responses to television.
In: Child Development, 50/1979/5, S. 41 – 45.
Bibl.; Tab.

*Children; Effects Research; Field Studies; Presentational Form;
Televiewing Frequency; Television; United States; Viewing Behavior*

339
Krull, Robert
Children learning to watch television.
In: Children's understanding of television.
Bryant, Jennings (Hrsg.) u.a.
New York, N.Y. u.a.: Academic Press 1983, S. 103 – 123.
Bibl.; Tab.

*Attention; Children; Literature Reviews; Program Formats; Reception
Processes; Television;*

340
Laosa, Luis M.
Viewing bilingual multicultural educational television. An empirical
analysis of children's behaviors during television viewing.
In: Journal of Educational Psychology, 68/1976/2, S. 133 – 142.
Bibl.; Tab.

*Bilingualism; Children; Cross Cultural Studies; Educational Television;
Imitation; Observation; Viewing Behavior; Visual Attention*

341
Noble, Grant
Sesame Street and Playschool revisited.
In: Media Information Australia, -/1983/28, S. 27 – 32.
Bibl.; Tab.

Attention; Australia; Children; Comparative Studies; Effects Research;
Participant Observation; "Sesame Street"; Viewing Behavior

342
Reid, Leonard N.; Frazer, Charles F.
Television at play.
In: Journal of Communication, 30/1980/4, S. 66 – 73.
Bibl.; Abb.

Children; Participant Observation; Peers; Play; Symbolic Interactionism;
Television; United States; Viewing Behavior

343
Rice, Mabel
What children talk about while they watch television.
Paper presented at the Biennial Meeting of the Southwestern Society for
Research in Human Development, Lawrence, Kan., March 1980.
Southwestern Society for Research in Human Development (Hrsg.)
Lawrence, Kan.: Univ. of Kansas 1980. 11 S. (Arlington, Va.: ERIC
ED 194 046.)
Bibl.; Tab.

Auditory Presentation; Children; Effects Research; Information
Processing; Reception Processes; Television; United States; Verbal
Behavior

344
Stoneman, Zolinda; Brody, Gene H.
Family interactions during three programs. Contextualist observations.
In: Journal of Family Issues, 4/1983/2, S. 349 – 365.
Bibl.; Tab.

Children; Effects Research; Family Relations; Participant Observation;
Program Realization; Television; United States

345
Winick, Mariann Pezzella; Winick, Charles
The television experience. What children see.
Beverly Hills, Calif. u.a.: Sage 1979. 212 S.
ISBN 0-8039-1143-2
Anm.; Tab.; Gph.

Adolescents; Adults; Age Differences; Children; Participant Observation; Reception Processes; Survey; Television; United States; Viewing Behavior

Chapter 11: Parental Influence and the Family

346
Atkin, Charles K.; Greenberg, Bradley S.
Parental mediation of children's social behavior learning from television.
Paper presented at the Annual Meeting of the Association for Education in Journalism, 60th, Madison, Wisconsin, August 1977.
Association for Education in Journalism (Hrsg.)
Madison, Wis.: Association for Education in Journalism 1977. 29 S.
(Arlington, Va.: ERIC ED 151 808.)
Bibl.; Tab.

Children; Effects Research; Mothers; Parent Influence; Prosocial Content; Questionnaires; Television; United States; Violent Content

347
Atkin, Charles K.; Miller, M. Mark
Parental mediation of children's television news learning.
In: Communications, 7/1981/1, S. 85 – 95.
Bibl.; Tab.

Attention; Children; Coviewing Adult; Knowledge Acquisition; Laboratory Experiments; News; Television; United States

348
Brody, Gene H.; Stoneman, Zolinda; Sanders, Alice K.
Effects of television viewing on family interactions. An observational study.
In: Family Relations, 29/1980/April, S. 216 – 220.
Bibl.; Tab.

Children; Family Relations; Observation; Parents; Recipient Behavior; Television; United States; Viewing Situation

349
Brown, John Ray
Child socialization. The family and television.
In: Der Anteil der Massenmedien bei der Herausbildung des Bewußtseins in der sich wandelnden Welt.
Leipzig: Karl-Marx-Universität, Sektion Journalistik 1975, S. 235 – 241.
Bibl.

Children; Family Relations; Mass Media; Socialization; Survey; Television; United Kingdom

350
Brown, J. Ray; Linné, Olga
The family as a mediator of television's effects.
In: Children and television.
Brown, J.Ray (Hrsg.)
London u.a.: Collier-Macmillan 1976, S. 184–198.
ISBN 02-977290-7
Bibl.; Anm.; Tab.

Children; Family Relations; Mass Media Effects; Television; Viewing Situation

351
Brown, J. Ray; Linné, Olga
Fernsehwirkungen und die Familie als Vermittlungsinstanz.
In: Wie Kinder mit dem Fernsehen umgehen.
Sturm, Hertha (Hrsg.) u.a.
Stuttgart: Klett-Cotta 1979, S. 199–213.
ISBN 3-12-930610-2
Bibl.; Anm.; Tab.

Children; Family Relations; Mass Media Effects; Television; Viewing Situation

352
Bryce, Jennifer W.; Leichter, Hope Jensen
The family and television. Forms and mediation.
In: Journal of Family Issues, 4/1983/2, S. 309–328.
Bibl.

Children; Effects Research; Family Relations; Intervening Variable; Learning Processes; Reception Processes; Television

353
Collins, W. Andrew; Sobol, Brian L.; Westby, Sally D.
Effects of adult commentary on children's comprehension and inferences about a televised aggressive portrayal.
In: Child Development, 52/1981/-, S. 158–163.
Bibl.; Tab.

Aggressive Behavior; Children; Comprehension; Coviewing Adult; Effects Research; Intervening Variable; Laboratory Experiments; Program Contents; Television; United States; Viewing Situation

354
Corder-Bolz, Charles R.
Meditation: the role of significant others.
In: Journal of Communication, 30/1980/3, S. 106–118.
Bibl.; Tab.

Academic Achievement; Children; Comparative Analysis; Comprehension;
Coviewing Adult; Mass Media Effects; Television

355
Davis, Dennis K.; Abelman, Robert
Families and Television. An application of frame analysis theory.
In: Journal of Family Issues, 4/1983/2, S. 385–404.
Bibl.

Children; Family; Learning Processes; Models; Parent Influence; Symbolic
Interactionism; Television

356
Dorr, Aimée
Interpersonal factors mediating viewing and effects.
In: Television as a teacher.
Coelho, George V. (Hrsg.)
Rockville, Md.: National Institute of Mental Health 1981, S. 61–82.
Bibl.

Adolescents; Children; Effects Research; Family Relations; Learning
Processes; Literature Reviews; Television; United States; Viewing Situation

357
Eron, Leonard D.
Parent-child interaction, television violence, and aggression of children.
In: American Psychologist, 37/1982/2, S. 197–211.
Bibl.; Tab.; Gph.

Aggressive Behavior; Children; Effects Research; Family Relations;
Intervening Variable; Longitudinal Studies; Program Preferences;
Television; United States; Violent Content

358
Esserman, June F.
A study of children's defenses against television commercial appeals.
In: Television advertising and children.
Esserman, June F. (Hrsg.) u.a.

New York, N.Y.: Child Research Service 1981, S. 43 – 54. (Arlington, Va.: ERIC ED 214 645.)
Bibl.; Tab.

Children; Cognitive Dissonance; Cognitive Processes; Laboratory Experiments; Parent Influence; Television Advertising; United States

359
Family contexts of television.
Leichter, Hope Jensen (Mitarb.); Ahmed, Durre (Mitarb.); Barrios, Leoncio (Mitarb.) u.a.
In: Educational Communication and Technology, 33/1985/1, S. 26 – 40.
Bibl.

Education; Family; Literature Reviews; Media Uses; Recipient Behavior; Television

360
Gross, Lynne Schafer; Walsh, Patricia R.
Factors affecting parental control over children's television viewing. A pilot study.
In: Journal of Broadcasting, 24/1980/3, S. 411 – 419.
Anm.

Children; Media Education; Parents; Survey; Television; United States; Viewing Behavior

361
Holman, J.; Braithwaite, V.A.
Parental lifestyles and children's television viewing.
In: Australian Journal of Psychology, 34/1982/3, S. 375 – 382.
Bibl.; Tab.

Attitudes; Australia; Children; Family Relations; Interviews; Parents; Recipient Behavior; Recreational Activities; Television; Viewing Behavior

362
Horton, Robert W.; Santogrossi, David A.
The effect of adult commentary on reducing the influence of televised violence.
In: Personality and Social Psychology Bulletin, 4/1978/2, S. 337 – 340.
Bibl.

Coviewing Adult; Laboratory Experiments; Prosocial Behavior; Students; Television; United States; Violent Content

363
Horton, Robert W.; Santogrossi, David A.
Mitigating the impact of televised violence through concurrent adult commentary.
Paper presented at the Annual Convention of the American Psychological Association, Toronto, Ontario, Canada, August 1978.
American Psychological Association (Hrsg.)
Toronto, Canada: APA 1978. 19 S. (Arlington, Va.: ERIC ED 177 412.)
Bibl.; Tab.

Children; Coviewing Adult; Effects Research; Intervening Variable; Laboratory Experiments; Parent Influence; Television; United States; Violent Content

364
Hunziker, Peter; Lüscher, Kurt; Fauser, Richard
Fernsehen im Alltag der Familie.
In: Rundfunk und Fernsehen, 23/1975/3 – 4, S. 284 – 315.
Bibl.; Tab.

Attitude Measurement; Children; Educational Attitudes; Federal Republic of Germany; Media Uses; Parents; Program Appreciation; Recipient Behavior; Recipient Research; Survey; Television

365
Hunziker, Peter
Fernsehen in der Familie. Eine Analyse der Gruppenstrukturen.
In: Fernsehen und Bildung, 11/1977/3, S. 269 – 285.
Bibl.; Tab.

Familiy Relations; Federal Republic of Germany; Group Structure; Parents; Reception Processes; Survey; Viewing Behavior; Television

366
Hunziker, Peter
Fernsehen und interpersonelle Kommunikation in der Familie.
In: Publizistik, 21/1976/2, S. 180 – 195.
Bibl.; Abb.

Family Relations; Reception Processes; Social Interaction; Television; Theory Formulation

367
Keeshan, Bob
Families and television.
In: Young Children, 38/1983/3, S. 46–55.
Bibl.; Abb.

Children; Education; Family; Mass Media Effects; Media Criticism; Television

368
Kohli, Martin
Die Bedeutung der Rezeptionssituation für das Verständnis eines Fernsehfilms durch Kinder. Eine experimentelle Pilot-Studie.
In: Zeitschrift für Soziologie, 5/1976/1, S. 38–51.
Bibl.; Tab.

Children; Effects Research; Empathy; Federal Republic of Germany; Intervening Variable; Laboratory Experiments; Mothers; Peers; Television; Viewing Situation

369
Korzenny, Felipe; Greenberg, Bradley S.; Atkin, Charles K.
Styles of parental disciplinary practices as a mediator of children's learning from antisocial television portrayals.
In: Communication yearbook. 3.
Nimmo, Dan (Hrsg.)
New Brunswick, N.J.: Transaction Books 1979, S. 283–293.
Bibl.; Tab.

Antisocial Behavior; Childrearing Practises; Children; Effects Research; Intervening Variable; Observational Learning; Parent Influence; Television; United States

370
Learning about the family from television.
Buerkel-Rothfuss, Nancy L. (Mitarb.); Greenberg, Bradley S. (Mitarb.); Atkin, Charles K. (Mitarb.) u.a.
In: Journal of Communication, 32/1982/3, S. 191–201.
Bibl.; Tab.

Attitude Formation; Children; Effects Research; Family; Parent Influence; Television; United States

371
Lometti, Guy; Feig, Ellen
Caring about children. The role of audience research.
In: Television and Children, 7/1984/1, S. 32 – 36.

*Anxiety; Arousal; Children; Mass Media Effects; Parent Influence;
Recipient Research; Summative Research; Television; United States;
Violent Content*

372
Lull, James
How families select television programs. A mass-observational study.
In: Journal of Broadcasting, 26/1982/4, S. 801 – 811.
Anm.; Tab.

*Family Relations; Fathers; Participant Observation; Program Preferences;
Recipient Research; Television; United States*

373
Lull, James
The social uses of television.
In: Human Communication Research, 6/1980/3, S. 198 – 209.
Bibl.

*Family Relations; Participant Observation; Recipient Behavior; Research
Needs; Television; United States; Uses and Gratifications*

374
Lull, James
The social uses of television.
In: Mass communication review yearbook. 3.
Whitney, Charles D. (Hrsg.) u.a.
Beverly Hills, Calif.: Sage 1982, S. 397 – 409.
Bibl.

*Family Relations; Participant Observation; Recipient Behavior; Research
Needs; Television; United States; Uses and Gratifications*

375
Messaris, Paul
Family conversations about television.
In: Journal of Family Issues, 4/1983/2, S. 293 – 308.
Bibl.

*Children; Communication Behavior; Family Relations; Recipient Research;
Television; United States*

376
Messaris, Paul; Kerr, Dennis
Mothers' comments about TV. Relation to family communication
patterns.
In: Communication Research, 10/1983/2, S. 175 – 194.
Bibl.; Tab.

Children; Communication Behavior; Coviewing Adult; Interviews;
Mothers; Television; Viewing Behavior; Viewing Situation; United States

377
Messaris, Paul; Sarett, Carla
On the consequences of television-related parent-child interaction.
In: Mass communication review yearbook. 3.
Whitney, Charles D. (Hrsg.) u.a.
Beverly Hills, Calif.: Sage 1982, S. 365 – 383.
Bibl.

Family Relations; Mass Media Effects; Media Literacy; Reality Perception;
Recipient Behavior; Research Needs; Social Behavior; Television; Theory
Formulation; Viewing Situation

378
Messaris, Paul; Kerr, Dennis
TV-related mother-child interaction and children's perceptions of TV
characters.
In: Journalism Quarterly, 61/1984/3, S. 662 – 666.
Anm.

Children; Family Relations; Generalization; Identification; Interviews;
Mothers; Parent Influence; Person Perception; Stereotype Portrayals;
Television; United States

379
Mohr, Phillip J.
Parental guidance of children's viewing of evening television programs.
In: Journal of Broadcasting, 23/1979/2, S. 213 – 228.
Anm.; Tab.

Children; Coviewing Adult; Interviews; Parents; Program Preference;
Television; United States

380
Mohr, Phillip J.
Television, children and parents. A report of the viewing habits, program

preferences, and parental guidence of school children in the fourth through the ninth grades in Sedgwick County, Kan., November 1976. State University, Wichita, Kan. (Hrsg.)
Wichita, Kan.: State Univ. 1977. ca. 483 S.
(Arlington, Va.: ERIC ED 158 730.)
Bibl.; Tab.; Kt.

Family Television Programs; Media Selection; Parent Influence; Program Preference; Questionnaires; Students; Televiewing Frequency; Television; United States

381
Prasad, V. Kanti; Rao, Tanniru R.; Sheikh, Anees A.
Mediating role of parental influence in children's response to television commercials. An exploratory study.
Paper presented at the Annual Meeting of the American Psychological Association, San Francisco, Calif., August 26 – 30, 1977.
American Psychological Association (Hrsg.)
San Francisco, Calif.: APA 1977. 20 S. (Arlington, Va.: ERIC ED 145 937.)
Bibl.; Gph.

Children; Effects Research; Laboratory Experiments; Parent Influence; Television Advertising; United States

382
Prasad, V. Kanti; Rao, Tanniru R.; Sheikh, Anees A.
Can people affect television? Mother versus commercial.
In: Journal of Communication. 28/1978/1, S. 91 – 96.
Bibl.; Tab.

Children; Effects Research; Laboratory Experiments; Mothers; Parent Influence; Television; United States

383
Reid, Leonard N.; Frazer, Charles F.
Children's use of television commercials to initiate social interaction in family viewing situations.
In: Journal of Broadcasting, 24/1980/2, S. 149 – 158.
Anm.

Children; Family; Participant Observation; Social Interaction; Television Advertising; United States; Viewing Situation

384
Reid, Leonard N.
The impact of family group interaction on children's understanding of
television advertising.
In: Journal of Advertising, 8/1979/3, S. 13 – 19.
Bibl.; Gph.

Children; Comprehension; Effects Research; Family Relations; Interviews;
Participant Observation; Television Advertising; United States

385
Reid, Leonard N.; Frazer, Charles F.
A sociological study of children's use of television commercials to initiate
social interaction in family group viewing situations.
Paper presented at the Annual Meeting of the Association for Education
in Journalism, 61st, Seattle, Washington, August 13 – 16, 1978.
Association for Education in Journalism (Hrsg.)
o.O.: o.Verl. 1978. 16 S. (Arlington, Va.: ERIC ED 159 726.)
Bibl.

Activity; Children; Family Relations; Parents; Participant Observation;
Recipient Behavior; Siblings; Television Advertising; United States

386
Reid, Leonard N.
Viewing rules as mediating factors of children's responses to commercials.
In: Journal of Broadcasting, 23/1979/1, S. 15 – 26.
Anm.; Tab.

Children; Effects Research; Participant Observation; Reception Processes;
Symbolic Interactionism; Television Advertising; United States; Viewing
Situation

387
Ridley-Johnson, Robyn; Cooper, Harris; Chance, June
The relation of children's television viewing to school achievement and
I.Q.
In: Journal of Educational Research, 76/1982/5, S. 294 – 297.
Bibl.; Tab.

Academic Achievement; Children; Coviewing Adult; Effects Research;
Intelligence; Interviews; Primary School; Television; United States;
Viewing Behavior

388
Robertson, Thomas S.
Parental mediation of television advertising effects.
In: Journal of Communication, 29/1979/1, S. 12 – 25.
Bibl.; Abb.

*Children; Effects Research; Family Relations; Intervening Variable;
Literature Reviews; Parent Influence; Television Advertising; Viewing
Situation*

389
Robertson, Thomas S.
Television advertising and parent-child relations.
In: The effects of television advertising on children.
Adler, Richard P. (Hrsg.) u.a.
Lexington, Mass, u.a.: Lexington Books 1981, S. 195 – 212.
Tab.

*Children; Communication Behavior; Conflict Resolution; Consumer
Behavior; Family Relations; Parents; Program Appreciation; Recipient
Research; Television Commercials; United States; Viewing Behavior*

390
Rossiter, John R.; Robertson, Thomas S.
Children's television viewing. An examination of parent-child consensus.
In: Sociometry, 38/1975/2, S. 308 – 326.
Bibl.; Tab.

*Children; Family Relations; Interviews; Parent Influence; Television;
United States*

391
Salomon, Gavriel
Effects of encouraging Israeli mothers to co-observe 'Sesame Street' with
their five-year-olds.
In: Child Development, 48/1977/-, S. 1146 – 1151.
Bibl.; Tab.

*Academic Achievement; Coviewing Adult; Effects Research; Field Studies;
Israel; Mothers; Preschool Children; "Sesame Street"; Social Status;
Televiewing Frequency*

392
Singer, Dorothy G.; Singer, Jerome L.
Family television viewing habits and the spontaneous play of preschool
children.
In: American Journal of Orthopsychiatry, 46/1976/3, S. 496 – 502.
Bibl.

*Effects Research; Laboratory Experiments; Media Education; Parents;
Play; Preschool Children; United States; Viewing Behavior; Viewing
Situation*

393
Singer, Jerome L.; Singer, Dorothy G.
Television viewing, family style and aggressive behavior.
Paper presented at the 1979 AAAS Annual Meeting, Houston, Texas.
Yale University, New Haven, Conn., Family Television Research and
Consultation Center (Mitarb.)
New Haven, Conn.: Yale Univ. 1979. 29 S.
Bibl.; Tab.

*Aggressive Behavior; Children; Effects Research; Family Relations;
Intervening Variable; Television; United States; Violent Content*

394
Streicher, Lawrence H.; Bonney, Norman L.
Children talk about television.
In: Journal of Communication, 24/1974/3, S. 54 – 61.
Bibl.; Abb.; Tab.

*Children; Interviews; Parent Influence; Program Preferences; Television;
United States*

395
Surlin, Stuart H.; Wurtzel, Alan; Whitener, Linda
Parental control of children's television viewing behavior. Support for the
reserve modeling principle.
Paper presented at the Annual Meeting of the International
Communication Association, Chicago, Ill. April 25 – 29, 1978.
International Communication Association (Hrsg.)
Chicago, Ill.: ICA, Mass Communication Division 1978. 16 S. (Arlington,
Va.: ERIC ED 157 122.)
Bibl.; Tab.

*Children; Educational Attainment; Media Selection; Parent Influence;
Survey; Television; Televiewing Frequency; United States*

396
Television and social relations: Family influence and consequences for
interpersonal behavior.
MacLeod, Jack M. (Mitarb.); Fitzpatrick, Mary Anne (Mitarb.); Glynn,
Carroll J. (Mitarb.) u.a.
In: Television and behavior. 2.
Pearl, David (Hrsg.) u.a.
Rockville, Md.: National Institute of Mental Health 1982, S. 272 – 286.
Bibl.

*Effects Research; Family Relations; Intervening Variable; Literature
Reviews; Social Interaction; Television; United States; Viewing Situation*

397
Walling, James I.
The effect of parental interaction on learning from television.
In: Communication Education, 25/1976/January, S. 16 – 24.
Anm.; Tab.

*Children; Effects Research; Family Relations; Identification; Interviews;
Parent Influence; Socialization; Television; United States*

398
Wiman, Alan R.
Parental influence and children's responses to television advertising.
In: Journal of Advertising, 12/1983/1, S. 12 – 18.
Bibl.; Tab.

*Attitude Formation; Children; Comprehension; Effects Research; Family
Relations; Intervening Variable; Parent Influence; Television; Television
Advertising; United States*

Chapter 12: Peers

399
Drabman, Ronald S.; Thomas, Margaret Hanratty
Children's imitation of aggressive and prosocial behavior when viewing
alone and in pairs.
In: Journal of Communication, 27/1977/3, S. 199 – 205.
Bibl.; Tab.

*Aggressive Behavior; Children; Effects Research; Imitation; Laboratory
Experiments; Peers; Prosocial Behavior; Television; United States; Viewing
Situation; Violent Content*

400
Effects of peer presence on preschool children's television-viewing
behavior.
Anderson, Daniel R. (Mitarb.); Lorch, Elizabeth Pugzles (Mitarb.); Smith,
Robin (Mitarb.) u.a.
In: Developmental Psychology, 17/1981/4, S. 446 – 453.
Bibl.; Tab.

*Distraction; Laboratory Experiments; Peers; Preschool Children; Recipient
Behavior; Social Interaction; Television; United States; Viewing Behavior;
Viewing Situation*

401
Frazer, Charles F.
The social character of children's television viewing.
In: Communication Research, 8/1981/3, S. 307 – 322.
Bibl.

*Children; Observation; Peers; Play; Recipient Behavior; Television; Social
Interactionism; United States*

402
Kohli, Martin
Die Bedeutung der Rezeptionssituation für das Verständnis eines
Fernsehfilms durch Kinder. Eine experimentelle Pilot-Studie.
In: Zeitschrift für Soziologie, 5/1976/1, S. 38 – 51.
Bibl.; Tab.

*Children; Effects Research; Empathy; Federal Republic of Germany;
Intervening Variable; Laboratory Experiments; Mothers; Peers; Television;
Viewing Situation*

403
Stoneman, Zolinda; Brody, Gene H.
Peers as mediators of television food advertisements aimed at children.
In: Developmental Psychology, 17/1981/6, S. 853 – 858.
Bibl.

Children; Children's Advertising; Consumer Behavior; Effects Research;
Food Advertising; Laboratory Experiments; Peers; Role Models;
Television; United States

Part IV: Media Education

Chapter 13: Media Education

404
Anderson, James A.
Television literacy and the critical viewer.
In: Children's understanding of television.
Bryant, Jennings (Hrsg.) u.a.
New York, N.Y. u.a.: Academic Press 1983, S. 297 – 330.
Bibl.; Anm.

Children; Educational Objectives; Media Education; Media Literacy;
Television; Theoretical Criticism; United States

405
Anderson, James A.
The theoretical lineage of critical viewing curricula.
In: Journal of Communication, 30/1980/3, S. 64 – 70.
Bibl.; Anm.; Abb.

Children; Curriculum; Media Education; Media Literacy; Parents; School;
Television; United States

406
Ashton, N. Craig
The way we see it. A program design for instruction of critical televiewing
skills.
In: Education for the television age.
Ploghoft, Milton E. (Hrsg.) u.a.
Springfield, Ill.: Thomas 1981, S. 55 – 63.

Children; Curriculum Development; Media Development; Media Literacy;
Primary School; Project Descriptions; Television; United States

407
Barthelmes, Jürgen; Herzberg, Irene; Nissen, Ursula
Kind und Fernsehen.
Deutsches Jugendinstitut, München (Hrsg.)
München: Bardtenschlager 1983. 196 S.

(Materialien für die medienpädagogische Aus- und Fortbildung von Erziehern. 1)
ISBN 3-7623-0104-2
Bibl.; Abb.; Tab.; Gph

Children; Federal Republic of Germany; Introductory Literature; Kindergartens; Mass Media Effects; Media Education; Parent Education; Television

408
Bilowit, Debbie Wasserman
Critical television viewing. A public television station reaches out.
In: Education for the television age.
Ploghoft, Milton E. (Hrsg.) u.a.
Springfield, Ill.: Thomas 1981, S. 64 – 70.

Media Education; Media Literacy; Primary School; Project Descriptions; Television; United States

409
Blickle, Ingrid; Friedl, Christa; Müller, Werner
Medienerziehung im Kindergarten.
In: Spiel und Medien in Familie, Kindergarten und Schule.
Meyer, Ernst (Hrsg.)
Heinsberg: Dieck 1984, S. 139 – 146.

Federal Republic of Germany; Kindergartens; Media Education; Preschool Children; Project Descriptions; Reception Processes; Television

410
Borchert, Manfred; Derichs-Kunstmann, Karin
Modell Medienverbund 'Immer dieses Fernsehen'.
Österreich. Bundesministerium für Unterricht und Kunst (Mitarb.);
Deutsche Lesegesellschaft (Mitarb.); Pestalozzianum, Zürich (Mitarb.)
Wien: TR-Verlagsunion; Ravensburg: Maier; Zug: Klett u. Balmer 1983.
89 S.
ISBN 3-215-05121-4; 3-473-60452-6; 3-264-90181-1
Anm.; Abb.

Adult Education; Austria; Federal Republic of Germany; Media Education; Media Systems; Supplementary Material; Switzerland; Television

411
Corder-Bolz, Charles R.
Development of critical television viewing skills in elementary school
students. Final report.
Southwest Educational Development Laboratory, Austin, Tex. (Hrsg.)
Austin, Tex.: Educational Development Lab. 1980. 234 S. (Arlington, Va.:
ERIC ED 215 671.)
Abb.; Tab.; Kt.

*Adolescents; Children; Curriculum Development; Longitudinal Studies;
Media Education; Media Literacy; Parents; Primary School; Project
Descriptions; Television; Teachers; United States*

412
Crowell, Doris C.
Educational technology research. Should we teach children how to learn
from television?
In: Educational Technology, -/1981/December, S. 18 – 22.
Bibl.; Abb.

*Children; Cognitive Processing; Comprehension; Effects Research; Media
Education; Media Literacy; Television; Testing; United States*

413
Donohue, Thomas R.; Henke, Lucy L.; Meyer, Timothy P.
Learning about television commercials. The impact of instructional units
on children's perceptions of motive and intent.
In: Journal of Broadcasting, 27/1983/3, S. 251 – 261.
Bibl.; Tab.

*Children; Cognitive Development; Comprehension; Laboratory
Experiments; Media Education; Television Advertising; United States*

414
Doolittle, John C.
Immunizing children against possible antisocial effects of viewing
television violence. A curricular intervention.
In: Perceptual and Motor Skills, 51/1980/2, S. 498.
Anm.

*Aggressive Behavior; Arousal; Children; Effects Research; Laboratory
Experiments; Media Education; Sex Differences; Television; United States;
Violent Content*

415
Dorr, Aimée; Graves, Sherryl Browne; Phelps, Erin
Television literacy for young children.
In: Journal of Communication, 30/1980/3, S. 71–83.
Bibl.; Anm.; Tab.

Academic Achievement; Age Differences; Children; Media Education;
Media Literacy; Perceptual Discrimination; Reality Perception; Television;
United States

416
Education for the television age. The proceedings of a national conference
on the subject of children and television.
Ploghoft, Milton E. (Hrsg.); Anderson, James A. (Hrsg.)
Springfield, Ill.: Thomas 1981. 183 S.
ISBN 0-398-04615-8
Bibl.; Anm.

Children; Cognition; Conference Proceedings; Media Education; Media
Literacy; Project Descriptions; Reception Processes; Television; United
States

417
Ellingsen, Melva
Television viewer skills project Eugene, Oregon School District.
In: Education for the television age.
Ploghoft, Milton E. (Hrsg.) u.a.
Springfield, Ill.: Thomas 1981, S. 88–90.

Media Education; Media Literacy; Project Descriptions; Secondary
School; Students; Television; United States

418
Furian, Martin
Kinder und Jugendliche vor dem Bildschirm. Hilfen zum Umgang mit dem
Medium.
In: Jugend und neue Medien – Hilfe vor dem Bildschirm.
Bonn: AGJ 1984, S. 57–74.

Adolescents; Children; Introductory Literature; Mass Media Effects;
Media Education; Television; Youth Policy

419
Furian, Martin; Maurer, Monika
Praxis der Fernseherziehung in Kindergarten, Hort, Heim und Familie.
Heidelberg: Quelle u. Meyer 1978. 139 S.
ISBN 3-494-00953-8
Bibl.; Anm.; Tab.; Gph.

Family; Kindergartens; Media Education; Media Uses; Parent Education; Reception Processes; Viewing Situation

420
Höltershinken, Dieter
Fernseherziehung im Kindergarten. Ein Ratgeber für Erzieher und Eltern
– auch in den ersten Grundschuljahren.
Verband Bildung und Erziehung (Hrsg.)
Köln: VBE 1982. 28 S.
(Beiträge zum Elementarbereich.)
ISBN 3-922975-09-7
Bibl.; Anm.; Abb.; Tab.; Gph.

Children; Educators; Introductory Literature; Media Education; Parents; Television

421
Höltershinken, Dieter
Mit Kindern fernsehen. Wie die Familie mit dem Fernsehen am besten umgeht.
Freiburg i.Br. u.a.: Herder 1979. 63 S.
(Elternziele.)
ISBN 3-451-18073-1
Bibl.; Abb.; Tab.

Children; Family; Mass Media Effects; Media Education; Television; Viewing Behavior

422
Immer dieses Fernsehen. Handbuch für den Umgang mit Medien.
Doelker, Christian (Hrsg.); Franzmann, Bodo (Hrsg.); Hartmann,
Waltraut (Hrsg.) u.a.
Wien: TR-Verlagsunion; Ravensburg: Maier; Zug: Klett u. Balmer 1983.
134 S.
ISBN 3-215-05113-3; 3-473-60451-8; 3-264-90180-3
Abb.

*Adult Education; Austria; Federal Republic of Germany; Mass Media
Effects; Media Education; Media Systems; Supplementary Material;
Switzerland; Television*

423
Kaye, Evelyn
The family guide to children's television. What to watch, what to miss,
what to change and how to do it.
Action for Children's Television, Boston, Mass. (Hrsg.); American
Academy of Pediatrics, Evanston, Ill. (Mitarb.)
New York: Pantheon 1974. XVIII, 194 S.
ISBN 0-394-49157-2; 0-394-70637-4

Children; Family; Media Education; Television

424
Kelmer, Otto; Stein, Arnd
Das Fernsehen und unsere Kinder. Ein Ratgeber für Eltern.
München: Kösel 1978. 127 S.
ISBN 3-466-34004-7

*Children; Introductory Literature; Mass Media Effects; Media Education;
Parent Education; Television*

425
Kinder und Medien. Was Kinder und Jugendliche mit Fernsehsendungen,
Radiosendungen und Zeitschriften machen können.
Plenz, Ralf (Hrsg.)
Hardebek: Eulenhof-Verlag Heinold 1981. 258 S.
(Bulletin Jugend und Literatur, Beiheft. 15)
ISBN 3-88710-002-6
Bibl.; Abb.; Tab.; Gph.

*Adolescents; Children; Compilations; Federal Republic of Germany;
Journals; Media Education; Radio; Recipient Participation; Television*

426
Klass, Karen
National Education Association activities in receivership skills curricula.
In: Education for the televison age.
Ploghoft, Milton E. (Hrsg.) u.a.
Springfield, Ill.: Thomas 1981, S. 106 – 110.

Media Education; Media Literacy; Parents; Project Descriptions;
Teachers; Television; United States

427
Lefold, Peter
Medienerziehung am Beispiel Fernsehen. Medienprojekt mit Kindern. Drei
Programme mit Fotos, Schmalfilmen und Tonbandaufnahmen.
Hannover u.a.: Schroedel 1980. 163 S.
(Schroedel elementar.)
ISBN 3-507-62060-X
Abb.

Children; Film; Media Education; Slides; Tape Recordings; Television

428
Lemon, Judith
Teaching children to become more critical consumers of television.
Paper presented at the Annual Meeting of the American Psychological
Association, Washington, D.C., September 5, 1976.
In: Children's critical evaluation of television content.
Leifer, Aimée Dorr (Hrsg.) u.a.
Cambridge, Mass.: Harvard Univ. 1976, 6 S.

Children; Media Education; Media Literacy; Television; United States

429
Lloyd-Kolkin, Donna; Wheeler, Patricia; Strand, Theresa
Developing a curriculum for teenagers.
In: Journal of Communication, 30/1980/3, S. 119 – 125.
Bibl.; Tab.; Abb.

Children; Curriculum Development; Media Education; Media Literacy;
Project Descriptions; Television; United States

430
Masterman, Len
Teaching about television.
London: Macmillan 1983. XV, 222 S.
ISBN 0-333-26677-3
Bibl.; Reg.; Abb.; Tab.

Curriculum; Media Education; Media Literacy; School; Television; United Kingdom

431
Medienpädagogik im Kindergarten. Überlegungen zur Arbeit mit Fernsehen und Film.
Barthelmes, Jürgen (Mitarb.); Heimbucher, Achim (Mitarb.); Herzberg, Irene (Mitarb.) u.a.
Deutsches Jugendinstitut, München, Arbeitsgruppe Vorschulerziehung (Hrsg.)
München: Verlag Deutsches Jugendinstitut 1978. 216 S.
(DJI Materialien.)
Bibl.

Compilations; Federal Republic of Germany; Kindergartens; Media Education; Media Pedagogics; Preschool Education; Socialization; Television

432
Mundzeck, Heike
Kinder lernen fernsehen. Was, wann, wie lange und wozu?
Reinbek b. Hamburg: Rowohlt 1973. 146 S.
(rororo Sachbuch. 6834)
ISBN 3-499-16834-0
Bibl.; Anm.; Abb.; Tab.

Children; Mass Media Effects; Media Education; Television

433
Mundzeck, Heike; Schneider, Wilfried
Praktische Medienerziehung. Fernsehen, Hörfunk, Programmzeitschrift –
Beispiele und Anregungen für Lehrer und Erzieher.
Weinheim u.a.: Beltz 1979. 151 S.
(Beltz-Praxis.)
ISBN 3-407-62023-3
Bibl.; Abb.

*Children; Educators; Media Education; Media Pedagogics; Project
Descriptions; Radio; Teachers; Television*

434
Neubauer, Wolfgang
Einführung in die Medienerziehung. Studientexte.
Köln: Verlagsgesellschaft Schulfernsehen 1982. 174 S.
(Medienpraxis – Medientheorie.)
ISBN 3-8025-8008-7
Bibl.; Reg.

*Auditory Media; Film; Indroductory Literature; Media Education; Printed
Material; Television; Theatre; Visual Media*

435
Neubauer, Wolfgang
Medienerziehung in der Grundschule.
Friedrich, Adelheid (Mitarb.); Schünemann, Dorothea (Mitarb.); Innerling,
Gudrun (Mitarb.) u.a.
Köln: Verlagsgesellschaft Schulfernsehen 1980. 172 S.
(Medienpraxis – Medientheorie.)
ISBN 3-8025-8013-3
Bibl.; Abb.; Tab.; Gph.

*Advertising; Comics; Media Education; Primary School; Radio; Students;
Television*

436
O'Bryant, Shirley L.; Corder-Bolz, Charles R.
Children and television. Tackling "the tube" with family teamwork.
In: Children Today, 7/1978/3, S. 21–24.
Anm.

*Mass Media Effects; Media Education; Media Uses; Parent Influence;
Preschool Children; Television; United States; Violent Content*

437
Perret, Daniel A.
Your child and play TV. Getting involved workshop guide. A manual for the parent group trainer.
Community Services for Children, Bethlehem, Pa. (Hrsg.)
Southwest Educational Development Laboratory, Austin, Tex. (Hrsg.)
Bethlehem, Pa.: Community Services for Children 1983. 55 S. (Arlington, Va.: ERIC ED 245 787.)
Abb.; Tab.

Children; Handbook; Media Education; Parent Education; Preschool Children; Television; United States

438
Perspectives on television education. Television Education Workshop: Multiculturalism Canada. Ottawa, Canada, February 26 – 28, 1981.
Ungerleider, Charles S. (Hrsg.); Thomas, Barb (Mitarb.); Collins, Joan (Mitarb.) u.a.
Canada, Minister of Supply and Services (Hrsg.)
Ottawa, Ont.: Information Canada 1981. 81 S.
(Arlington, Va.: ERIC ED 217 865.)
Bibl.; Abb.

Adolescents; Canada; Children; Conference Proceedings; Media Education; Media Literacy; Television; United States

439
Pierre, Evelyne
A French experiment in educating young television viewers.
In: Prospects, 13/1983/2, S. 235 – 242.

Adolescents; Field Studies; France; Media Education; Reception Processes; Students; Television

440
Pierre, Evelyne; Chagiuboff, Jean; Chapelain, Brigitte
Les nouveaux téléspectateurs de neuf à dix-huit ans. Entretiens et analyses.
Programme interministériel "Jeunes téléspectateurs actifs".
Institut National de l'Audiovisuel, Paris (Hrsg.)

Paris: La Documentation Française 1982. 224 S.
(Audiovisuel et communication.)
ISBN 2-11-000814-8

Adolescents; Attitude Formation; Field Studies; France; Learning Processes; Media Education; Media Literacy; Reality Perception; Reception Processes; Students; Television; Viewing Situation

441
Ploghoft, Milton E.; Anderson, James A.
Teaching critical television viewing skills. An integrated approach.
Springfield. Ill.: Thomas 1982. IX, 192 S.
ISBN 0-398-04616-6
Bibl.; Reg.; Tab.

Children; Media Education; Media Literacy; Practical Relevance; Television

442
Potter, Rosemary Lee
New season. The positive use of commercial television with children.
Columbus, Ohio: Merrill 1976. IX, 126 S.
ISBN 0-675-08625-6
Bibl.; Reg.; Abb.

Children; Commercial Television; Media Education; Television Advertising; United States

443
Reid, Leonard N.
Regulating children's television advertising. Reassessing parental responsibility.
Paper presented at the Annual Meeting of the Association for Education in Journalism, Seattle, Wash., August 23 – 16, 1978.
Association for Education in Journalism (Hrsg.)
East Lansing, Mich.: Michigan State Univ. 1978. 12 S. (Arlington, Va.: ERIC ED 159 679.)
Bibl.

Children; Consumer Education; Coviewing Adult; Effects Research; Media Education; Parent Influence; Television Advertising; United States

444
Retter, Hein
Antifernseh-Fibel. Kindererziehung ohne Fernsehen – Anstiftung zu
einem fernsehfreien Familienleben.
Bamberg: Wenos 1981. 115 S.
ISBN 3-922926-00-2
Bibl.

*Children; Family Relations; Media Criticism; Media Education; Media
Effects; Television*

445
Schaff, Suzanne
Television receivership skills program in the East Syracuse-Minoa Central
Schools.
In: Education for the television age.
Ploghoft, Milton E. (Hrsg.) u.a.
Springfield, Ill.: Thomas 1981, S. 85 – 87.

*Media Education; Media Literacy; Project Descriptions; Secondary
School; Students; Television; United States*

446
Schneller, Raphael; Gan, Ramat
Training for critical TV viewing.
In: Educational Research, 24/1982/2, S. 99 – 106.
Bibl.; Tab.

*Attitude Change; Children; Credibility; Israel; Laboratory Experiments;
Media Education; Media Literacy; News; Television*

447
Singer, Dorothy G.; Zuckerman, Diana M.; Singer, Jerome L.
Helping elementary school children learn about TV.
In: Journal of Communication, 30/1980/3, S. 84 – 93.
Bibl.; Abb.

*Academic Achievement; Children; Family Relations; Media Education;
Media Literacy; Television; United States; Viewing Behavior*

448
Singer, Dorothy G.; Singer, Jerome L.
Learning how to be intelligent consumers of television.
In: Learning from television.
Howe, Michael J.A. (Hrsg.) u.a.
London u.a.: Academic Press 1983, S. 204 – 222.
Bibl.

Children; Curriculum Research; Media Education; Media Literacy;
Reading; School; Stereotype; Televiewing Frequency; Television; United
States

449
Singer, Dorothy G.; Zuckerman, Diana M.; Singer, Jerome L.
Teaching elementary school children critical television viewing skills. An
evaluation.
In: Education for the television age.
Ploghoft, Milton E. (Hrsg.) u.a.
Springfield, Ill.: Thomas 1981, S. 71 – 81.
Bibl.

Children; Media Education; Media Literacy; Primary School; Project
Descriptions; Television; United States

450
Singer, Dorothy G.; Singer, Jerome L.; Zuckerman, Diana M.
Teaching television. How to use TV to your child's advantage.
New York, N.Y.: The Dial Press 1981. XIII, 209 S.
ISBN 0-8037-8515-1

Children; Heavy Viewer; Media Pedagogics; Television; Textbook; United
States

451
Television awareness training. The viewer's guide for family and
community.
Logan, Ben (Hrsg.); Moody, Kate (Hrsg.)
New York, N.Y.: Media Action Research Center 1979. 280 S.
ISBN 0-918084-02-4
Bibl.; Reg.; Tab.

Children; Compilations; Family; Media Education; Television

452
Wartella, Ellen
Television watching as an information processing task. Programming and advertising.
Paper presented at the Annual Meeting of the American Psychological Association, New York, N.Y., Sepember 1 – 5, 1979.
American Psychological Association (Hrsg.); Institute of Communication Research, Champaign, Ill. (Hrsg.)
Urbana-Champaign, Ill.: Univ. of Illinois 1979. 16 S. (Arlington, Va.: ERIC ED 180 607.)
Bibl.; Tab.

Academic Achievement; Consumer Education; Educators; Media Education; Media Literacy; Persuasive Communication; Preschool Children; Television Advertising; United States

453
Weber, David M.
The effects of critical television viewing in educating primary students. An annotated bibliography.
South Bend, Ind.: Indiana Univ. 1982. 38 S. (Arlington, Va.: ERIC ED 218 011.)
Bibl.

Bibliography; Children; Media Education; Media Literacy; Television

454
Young, Marion R.
The P.T.A. critical viewing skills project.
In: Education for the television age.
Ploghoft, Milton E. (Hrsg.) u.a.
Springfield, Ill.: Thomas 1981, S. 111 – 115.

Children; Media Education; Project Descriptions; Television; United States

Author Index

U

Ungerleider, Charles S. 438
United States, Dept. of Health
  and Human Services 70, 71, 73
University of Kansas 329
University of Massachusetts 204
University of Minnesota 285
University of North Carolina 310
University of Toronto 109

V

Vance, Donald 245
Verband Bildung und Erziehung
  420
Verna, Mary Ellen 9, 10
Vibbert, Martha M. 246
Vitouch, Peter 192

W

Wackman, Daniel B. 247, 248,
  249, 253
Wahlroos, Carita 193
Wakshlag, Jacob J. 123
Walling, James J. 397
Walsh, Patricia R. 360
Ward, Scott 247, 249, 253
Wartella, Ellen 27, 103, 124, 125,
  142, 168, 178-182, 207, 225,
  237, 247, 248, 250, 253, 303,
  311, 452
Watkins, Bruce A. 92, 116, 219,
  220, 252
Watkins, Thomas A. 120
Watt, James H. 127, 128, 129
Weber, David M. 18, 453
Welch, Alicia J. 127, 128, 129

Wellman, Henry M. 133, 148
Wendelin, Carola 193
Werner, Peter 242
Westby, Sally Driscoll 145, 206,
  295, 297, 353
Wetstone, Harriet S. 153
Wheeler, Patricia 429
Whitener, Linda 395
Whitney, Charles D. 374, 377
Wilder, Paula Gillen 183, 184,
  216, 265, 307
Wilhoit, G. Cleveland 59, 179
Williams, Tannis MacBeth 251
Wilson, Barbara J. 187
Wiman, Alan R. 398
Winick, Charles 345
Winick, Mariann Pezzella 345
Winn, Marie 78, 79
Withey, Stephan B. 35
Wolf, Michelle A. 80, 328
Wright, John C. 93, 98-100, 113,
  117-119, 130, 139, 154, 167-169
  185, 198, 214, 252, 329
Wurtzel, Alan 395

Y

Yale University 393
Young, Marion R. 454

Z

Ziegler, Mark 131
Zillmann, Dolf 88, 123, 199, 200
Zuckerman, Diana M. 327, 447,
  449, 450
Zuckerman, Paul 69, 131
Zuckernick, Arlene 110
Zweites Deutsches Fernsehen 38

Subject Index

152

Parent Education 407, 419, 424, 437
Parent Influence 40, 67, 293, 347, 355, 358, 363, 369-371, 378, 380-382, 388, 390, 394, 395, 397, 398, 436, 443
Parent Participation 66, 279, 318
Parents 38, 347, 348, 360, 361, 364, 365, 379, 385, 389, 392, 405, 411, 420, 426
Participant Observation 11, 163, 164, 193, 266, 267, 291, 336, 341, 342, 344, 345, 372-374, 383-386
Peers 81, 131, 195, 292, 342, 368, 399-403
Perception 65, 222, 227, 248
Perceptual Development 27, 103, 142, 185, 265, 298
Perceptual Discrimination 210, 211, 216, 221, 222, 228, 245, 254, 256, 258-260, 262, 265-269, 271-276, 279, 291, 298, 317, 321, 415
Person Perception 35, 60, 110, 146, 183, 215, 246, 266, 280, 283, 284, 287, 289-291, 298, 299, 302-304, 306, 307, 378
Personality Traits 300, 301
Persuasive Communication 180, 182, 226, 228, 452
Piaget, J. 186, 202, 217, 241-244, 309
Play 67, 91, 93, 183, 331, 342, 392, 401
Political Socialization 17, 21, 58
Practical Relevance 63, 232, 233, 312, 325, 441
Preconceptions 147
Preschool Children 7, 45, 53, 54, 67, 81, 86, 91, 93, 95, 115, 121, 122, 128, 129, 152, 153, 155,
171, 175, 176, 178, 183, 184, 193, 198, 213, 215, 216, 221, 231, 253, 256, 258, 265, 266, 269, 278, 291, 307, 309, 329, 391, 392, 400, 409, 436, 437, 452
Preschool Education 75, 431
Presentational Form 89, 95, 109, 112, 114, 115, 118, 120, 121, 134, 137, 151-153, 158, 161, 168, 172, 180, 182, 187, 197, 199, 203, 213, 225, 230, 236, 237, 243, 244, 252, 258, 278, 298, 332, 338
Prevention 63
Primary School 327, 387, 406, 408, 411, 435, 449
Printed Material 241, 434
Professional Criticism 80, 97, 323
Prognosis 43
Program Appreciation 110, 132, 311, 364, 389
Program Contents 16, 25, 40, 106, 110, 145, 159, 189, 190, 194, 212, 222, 263, 274, 276, 277, 296, 311, 337, 353
Program Effectiveness 121, 152
Program Evaluation 75
Program Extension 68
Program Formats 101, 215, 216, 221, 245, 329, 339
Program Output 19, 50
Program Preferences 19, 34, 266, 291, 337, 357, 372, 379, 380, 394
Program Realization 82, 84, 344
Program Series 108
Project Descriptions 317, 327, 406, 408, 409, 411, 416, 417, 426, 429, 433, 445, 449, 454
Prosocial Behavior 277, 278, 294, 362, 399

158

COMMUNICATION RESEARCH AND BROADCASTING

A publication series of the
Internationales Zentralinstitut
für das Jugend- und Bildungsfernsehen

No. 1
School Radio in Europe
A documentation with
contributions given at the
European School Radio
Conference Munich 1977
1979. 198 pages. DM 28,–
ISBN 3-598-20200-8

No. 2
**Effects and Functions of
Television: Children and
Adolescents**
A bibliography of selected
research literature
1970–1978
Compiled by Manfred
Meyer and Ursula Nissen
1979. 172 pages. DM 28,–
ISBN 3-598-20201-6

No. 3
**Women, Communication,
and Careers**
Ed. by Marianne Grewe-
Partsch and Gertrude J.
Robinson
1980. 138 pages. DM 28,–
ISBN 3-598-20202-4

No. 4
Hertha Sturm, Sabine Jörg
**Information Processing by
Young Children**
Piaget's Theory of Intellec-
tual Development applied
to Radio and Television
1981. 95 pages. DM 24,–
ISBN 3-598-20204-0

No. 5
**Health Education by
Television and Radio**
Contributions to an Inter-
national Conference with
a Selected Bibliography
Edited by Manfred Meyer
1981. 476 pages. DM 42,–
ISBN 3-598-20203-2

No. 6
**Children and the Formal
Features of Television**
Approaches and Findings
of Experimental and
Formative Research
Ed. by Manfred Meyer
1983. 333 pages. DM 42,–
ISBN 3-598-20205-9

K·G·Saur München · New York · London · Paris

K·G·Saur Verlag KG · Postfach 71 10 09 · 8000 München 71 · Tel. (089) 79 89 01
K·G·Saur Inc. · 175 Fifth Avenue · New York, N.Y.10010 · Tel. (212) 982-1302
K·G·Saur Ltd. · Shropshire House · 2-10 Capper Street · London WC 1E 6JA · Tel. 01-637-1571
K·G·Saur, Editeur SARL. · 6, rue de la Sorbonne · 75005 Paris · Téléphone 354 47 57